Auras

Auras

How to balance and cleanse your energy body

Hamraz Ahsan

SIRIUS

For my darling daughter, Pawan.

Photos courtesy of Shutterstock.

SIRIUS

This edition published in 2021 by Sirius Publishing, a division of
Arcturus Publishing Limited,
26/27 Bickels Yard, 151–153 Bermondsey Street,
London SE1 3HA

ISBN: 978-1-3988-1322-9
AD008213US

Printed in China

Contents

Introduction

When I wrote my novel *Kabuko the Djinn* I drew on certain meditative practices I had engaged in for several years. Those practices had, over time, enabled me to explore what the energies in a human body look and feel like. I used that knowledge to write about the invisible forces that are housed within each of us. This is the closest I could get to describing what I saw within a human being's energy body: "Such vibrant colors, so much happening all at once—light dancing, snaking, leaping, bursts of energy and rivers of light everywhere." That description attempts to introduce the reader to the dynamic and wondrous body of light that lives inside our dense physical body. It is usually not possible to see that energy body with the naked eye. However, as I hope to show you in this book, you regularly sense those energies, even if you have never seen them.

For example, have you ever met someone and taken an instant dislike to them, before they've said or done anything? Conversely, have you met someone and known within seconds that you'll get along? Have you ever entered a house and felt like it was unwelcoming, or one where you immediately felt at home and never wanted to leave? These are all examples of your energy body giving you feedback on the people you meet and the places you enter.

The idea of invisible energies has been with us since time immemorial. For example, we know that prehistoric peoples used musical instruments and their own voices in ceremonies intended to help with the uncertainties of human life. These sounds—unlike music for entertainment purposes—were designed to activate the manifestation powers of the vibrational body. Since these were preliterate societies, it's impossible to say for sure if the modern understanding of the energy body popular in spiritual circles was the same for those early people. However, in calling for help from unseen forces—be they spirits or gods—our ancestors were stepping into the realm of energy, hidden from sight but definitely there.

A devotee dances at the shrine in Lahore, Pakistan, of Sufi saint, Shah Madhu Lal Hussain. His fingers indicate that he is becoming 'one' with divine energy within the trance dance.

The tradition I follow, that of Sufism, believes that we experience the divine when our energy body is in alignment with the vibrational force of the universe. This can be achieved by chanting the 99 names of God. It can also be achieved through dance, such as the whirling dervishes of Turkey or the *dhamal* (trance dance) practice of the devotees at Sufi shrines in the Indian subcontinent. For a person not following a particular tradition, meditation can also give rise to the same benefits of vibrational entrainment with divine energy.

In this book, you will find an understanding of your energetic structure, how to ensure that it is functioning at its optimal level, and how you can begin to understand the auras of those around you. This will help you in many practical ways in your daily life. It can ensure that you attract the best people and the best outcomes to you. It can help you decide whether you should work with a particular client, or if you should walk away from a project. When you are perfectly aligned energetically, with a clean, clear aura, you can live a life that is to your highest good.

'If the Milky Way were not within me,
how should I have seen it or known it?'
Kahlil Gibran

CHAPTER 1

What are auras?

The history of auras

Aura means "breeze" or "breath" in the ancient Greek language, and was also the name of a lesser-known Greek Titan goddess. The word's use as a name for the part of the energy sheath (visible to some adepts) outside the physical body came into being around the end of the 19th century. This latter meaning, of a sort of halo surrounding the body, was made particularly popular in the West by the theosophists. Theosophy is a school of philosophical thought founded in the late 19th century that focuses on examining the truth of the nature of the world and spirituality. It draws on aspects of wisdom found in Hinduism, Buddhism and Western esoteric thought. The movement has so many aspects to its practice that it would take another book to fully explore it all. However, for our purposes, we should look at the work of a theosophist called Charles Webster Leadbeater.

Leadbeater wrote extensively on the makeup of the human energy body, as well as doing some very detailed sketches of his idea of what chakras (energy points) in the body look like. He drew on some ideas from the Indian subcontinent alongside his own experiences of seeing energy after having done a number of meditation practices. This work was then used as the basis of an exploration into the subject in the late 1970s by Christopher Hills. The classic seven-chakra, rainbow-colored system that you may be familiar with is the result of the work Hills did in that decade. We will look at two chakra systems in more detail in chapter two (pages 36–63).

Beyond the work of 19th-century theosophy luminaries, we have little historical literature on auras as we know them today. However, it has been speculated that the halos shown around the heads of religious figures in Christian iconography could be there to indicate the radiant purity of their auras. Certainly the spirit or soul has been written about extensively, and some of the ideas we have of what remains after we die can be attributed to an energy body, if not precisely to an aura.

Author W.E. Butler wrote in his work *How to Read the Aura* that: "It is said in the East that the spiritual aura of the Lord Gautama Buddha extended for two hundred miles, and they also say that the whole of this

planet is held in the aura of a very great Being." Could it be that the more spiritually advanced we get, our auras become beacons of radiant joy for the world around us?

This mosaic of Christ in the arms of the Virgin Mary shows both with halos around their heads. There are those who believe that this is to show the purity of their auras.

Everything is responsive

Huna is a life philosophy from Hawaii that has many beneficial ideas about the world around us. Serge Kahili King, a Huna practitioner, has spoken about a number of principles governing the nature of reality. Among them is one that is very important and useful to anyone interested in auras: "everything is alive and responsive." Everything has an aura, irrespective of whether it is animate or inanimate. It used to be thought likely that only living beings had an energetic aura, but many esoteric practitioners have now confirmed that all matter has an aura. If you stub your toe on a cupboard, it may well be that your aura and that of the cupboard are not in harmony, and the stubbed toe is the outcome. (Although, it may just be that you need to move the cupboard to a less inconvenient spot!)

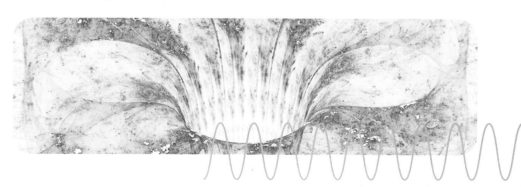

If we accept that everything has an aura, and that this aura is in constant interplay with all the other auras of things, people and places with which it interacts, then you can see how important it is to ensure that you only have around you those auras that you align well with.

PRAISE, DON'T CRITICIZE

One of the key ways in which Huna practitioners, in the tradition followed by Serge Kahili King, acknowledge the principle that everything is alive and responsive is to praise rather than criticize. This is a good way to come into harmony with all the auras of what surrounds you. A typical day might involve frustration when something doesn't work quite right. The coffee maker might not work the first time, or the shower might not get hot because the water heater isn't working properly. This might cause you to internally (or even externally) criticize and curse the inanimate objects involved and the overall quality of your life. This will immediately put you into disharmony in both your energy body and your physical experience. It is always far better to praise or to acknowledge things that do go right. How fortunate we are to have coffee makers, hot water and indoor plumbing that gives us an abundance of flowing water.

It is unrealistic to be positive all the time, even when things are going wrong, but maintaining an "attitude of gratitude" helps you to keep your auric energy clear and encourage the auras of the things and people around you to also vibrate at that higher level. You will find, over time, that life runs far more smoothly and happily.

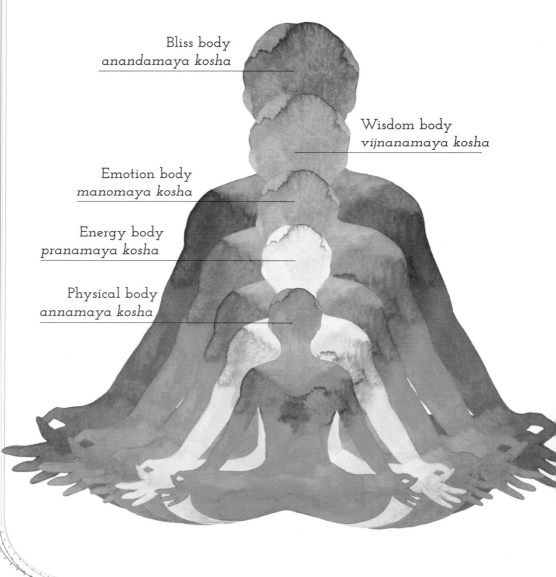

Self
brahman

Bliss body
anandamaya kosha

Wisdom body
vijnanamaya kosha

Emotion body
manomaya kosha

Energy body
pranamaya kosha

Physical body
annamaya kosha

Energetic sheaths

Different traditions believe energy is ordered in a variety of ways within the body. Some systems believe there are seven energy bodies radiating out from the skin, each concerned with a different aspect of your physical, emotional, intellectual and spiritual makeup. However, in Vedantic philosophy there are five koshas (sheaths) in the body that surround the eternal self, called the *brahman* or *atman* in the Advaita Vedanta. These sheaths each have an important role to play in keeping a person happy and healthy; they also interact with each other so that damage to one sheath will inevitably affect all the others.

You can find out more about how to restore each of the five koshas to optimum health on pages 20–24. Once you have cleared each of these five energy sheaths, you can maintain overall health by just working with one sheath, which represents all of them. If one visualizes a core, single sheath and concentrates one's efforts on keeping this clear and strong, the health of all the layers of the energy body is maintained. As such, we shall call this composite energy field the protective sheath.

THE PROTECTIVE SHEATH

The protective sheath reflects the energy of our current day-to-day life. If you could view it (and the meditation on pages 126–128 will show you how to practice doing this), you would see an ever-swirling, moving mist of color at the outer edge of the shape of things and people. Those changes in the energy body can happen because of your fluctuating emotions, hormonal changes, your interactions with others and your thoughts and beliefs about yourself and others.

When this sheath is working well, your intuition will be strong about situations and other people. You will see their motivations clearly and, for some, it is almost as if you have a psychic ability to know what's coming your way. That is because you do! This sheath, which has all the qualities

of the koshas, affects your psychic abilities keenly, and working to keep it clear and healthy is a good way to stay psychically alert.

If this sheath is damaged or weak, you can be left open to psychic attack. This is when you begin to attract unwelcome experiences to you, and life begins to have an increasing level of frustration to it. By working to strengthen this sheath, you can ensure you only attract those experiences to you that work for your highest good and make you feel positive and blissful about life.

CLEANSING THE ANNAMAYA KOSHA

The annamaya kosha is also known as the physical body, or the food sheath. This is because it is your physical self, which comprises what you eat and this corporeal body, that will become food for the Earth and its creatures, once your *atman,* or soul, has left this plane of existence.

It is therefore natural that the best way to cleanse and protect this part of your energetic makeup is good nutrition and maintaining excellent physical health. You may think that the physical is not as important as the spiritual when it comes to auras, but this is not true. You reside in your body, and any discomfort here will affect all your energy sheaths.

While it is beyond the scope of this book to advise on diet, it would be beneficial to look into booking an ayurvedic session to understand your specific body type and which foods will support your overall physical health. As a general rule of thumb for everyone, avoiding processed foods and veering toward whole, organically produced foods is best.

You can also cleanse this part of your auric body through exercise. However, be aware that the third leg of the tripod of physical health is relaxation, so do not undertake overly strenuous exercise. You can find some helpful yoga *asanas* to do on pages 70–87.

CLEANSING THE PRANAMAYA KOSHA

Pranamaya is the kosha that pertains to energy, since *prana* means energy. It is the vital energy that courses through the meridians or *nadis* of your body. This energy intersects at certain points called chakras, which we will learn more about in the next chapter (see pages 36–63).

If this energy sheath is not operating at full health, you will suffer from breathing problems and may lose your sense of smell or experience chronic fatigue. Working with the breath is the best way to cleanse this kosha. A daily breathing practice is recommended for all people as being as necessary as brushing your teeth in the morning.

You can do the alternate nostril breathing exercise on pages 72–73 as a quick and easy way to bring this sheath into alignment. Not only does this exercise restore the workings of this kosha, it also balances the "male" and "female" energies in the body, so you physically experience equilibrium. It does not matter what sex or gender you are, or how you identify yourself at all, as this is a cosmic duality at play that resides in all matter, irrespective of how it is presented biologically—we all have masculine and feminine energy as a dual experience within us which is usually resolved into one at the point of death or enlightenment.

CLEANSING THE MANOMAYA KOSHA

Have you ever heard the saying "energy flows to where attention goes"? This sheath, which is often called the mental or the emotional body kosha, shows the truth of that saying. Your emotions (the "energy" part of the saying) arise from your thoughts (the "attention" part of the saying), and those emotions have a direct influence on your health. Medical researchers have found that those with a positive outlook on life and optimistic thoughts live longer, healthier lives than those who are negative and pessimistic. So one of the best ways to cleanse and protect this sheath is to think good thoughts. Think well of people and, as seen on page 15, praise and don't criticise the world around you.

Another way to heal this sheath is to do anything that stops you from overthinking, so meditation, chanting and restorative yoga poses are all good for this. Since the way we think is often formed in childhood, it is very good to do the yoga *asana* Child's Pose (see pages 84–85). This helps us stop dwelling on, and feeling emotionally hurt by, thoughts of conflict or injustice. If you can put aside ideas that are causing you pain, you will heal this body and send vibrations of joy throughout your whole energy system.

CLEANSING THE VIJNANAMAYA KOSHA

This is where your intuition, wisdom and inspiration reside. Damage to this kosha will cause you to doubt yourself, feel unconnected to your spiritual truth, and give rise to depression and despair.

Mindfulness can help heal this sheath, since we are going beyond the world of rationality to a place of being the timeless "witness." This is the eternal part of yourself, the Buddha mind, that observes without judgment or attachment.

If you find that meditation or mindfulness does not work for you, you could try more traditional talking therapies to resolve problems in your Manomaya kosha, which will then affect the Vijnanamaya. The important thing is to go beyond the physical and to your own sense of spiritual awareness. This is the case even on a secular level, as you do not need to follow any religious or spiritual tradition to understand that energy is more than what we see in the material world. Take a quantum physics class if you really want to get a scientific understanding of what spiritual traditions have been saying about energy for millennia.

CONNECTING TO THE ANANDAMAYA KOSHA

This is called the Bliss body because when you understand experientially that we are all one connected energy manifesting in different forms, that realization is a blissful feeling. You may have felt this sensation when you are in a state of complete absorption in what you are doing, as described by psychologist Mihaly Csikszentmihalyi in his groundbreaking book *Flow*. You experience complete connection to what you are doing, and your thoughts and the ego are no longer calling the shots. You can also experience this feeling spontaneously through meditation practices. It takes time and practice to get to that feeling, but it is achievable and, once experienced, it becomes easier to tap back into it.

You do not really "cleanse" or heal this kosha, because it is always perfect. But problems in other sheaths can cause the connection between this part of our energy body to become disconnected from the rest. You can reconnect by doing charitable works that permit you to see that the people you are helping are no different from you. Once we understand *spiritually*, rather than intellectually, that we are all one, we connect to the bliss of this kosha.

Cleansing the protective sheath

Once you have thought about cleansing and connecting with your five koshas, you can simply maintain your energetic health by concentrating your efforts on the sum of those sheaths and visualizing it as a single protective sheath. There are several ways to cleanse this sheath. I recommend you do at least one a day and, ideally, create a monthly routine that incorporates all the suggestions below.

SMUDGING

Burning bundles of dried herbs is a tried-and-tested way to clear not just your own aura but the aura of the space around you. This is because your senses are a great conduit to your energy body. The scent of the herbs burning helps you feel transported to a more spiritual space in which you can visualize healing your body—both physical and energetic.

You can buy ready-made smudging sticks in alternative health shops, or you can make your own with bundles of dried herbs. Just make sure you have a fireproof dish available to catch any stray embers. Light the bundle, blow it out so that the end is smoking, and pass whatever you're smudging through the fragrant smoke. You can smudge your own aura by starting at your feet and moving the smoke up the left-hand side of your body, over the top of your head and down your right-hand side. Once you've finished, make sure you extinguish the smudgestick completely.

Herbs to smudge with:

- ❖ sage
- ❖ thyme
- ❖ rosemary
- ❖ cedar
- ❖ mugwort

SALT BATHS

Salt has long been considered a sacred substance—the taste of our tears, our bodies, the sea and the earth. Salt is also immensely cleansing and can be used to cleanse an aura easily and quickly. Whenever you feel particularly down or tired, simply take a couple of handfuls of one of the salts below and add them to a warm bath. When sitting in the bath, visualize the saltwater

sparkling with a cleansing light, and be sure to pass the water over your head and rub some of it on your belly button.

Salts to use:

- ❖ Epsom salt (this is not a salt in the sense of the others listed, but has many additional health benefits)
- ❖ Sea salt
- ❖ Himalayan pink salt
- ❖ Rosemary-infused salts
- ❖ Black salt (also called Kala Namak)

CHANTING

The right sounds can be very cleansing to your aura, especially when the sounds are reverberating through your body. As we will see in chapter two (pages 36–63), there are sounds connected to cleansing each chakra in the seven-chakra system, but there are also chants you can do that relate to a general aura cleansing without reference to a specific chakra. Try *Aah-Ummn* as a chant, opening your mouth like an O initially and then closing it and feeling the hum of the last part of the sound against your lips. Always prepare for your chant sessions by bathing, sitting in a clean room and, perhaps, lighting some incense if you like the smell of it. If you begin to feel light-headed, stop chanting, stamp your feet on the ground and rub your palms against your thighs. Chanting suits some people, but not everyone. So if you find you get headaches, earaches or feel dizzy after chanting, choose another method of aura cleansing.

DRINK WATER

This may sound like a ridiculous suggestion, but one way in which your aura will weaken considerably is if you are not adequately hydrated. Your physical body impacts your aura, which is why certain clairvoyants can "see" illnesses in a person's aura. When you are physically healthy, you have a far greater chance of keeping your aura clear and balanced. So drink at least eight glasses of water a day and remember that you will need more on hotter days when you sweat out a lot of water.

BODY MASSAGE

One of the most enjoyable ways of clearing your aura is massage with appropriate oils. You can ask a partner or family member to give you a massage or you can massage yourself. One of the best areas to massage is your feet. This is because they connect you to the earth and are a key area for strengthening your aura. After washing them, anoint them with oil and massage from the heel up to the toes—and remember to massage between your toes as well. Be careful if you're doing this on a slippery surface, and perhaps put socks on immediately afterwards to allow the oil to sink into your feet. If you're using essential oils, make sure you use a base oil, such as almond or coconut, so that you're not applying strong oils straight onto your skin.

Oils to use:

- ❖ rose oil to feel loved and supported
- ❖ basil oil to attract prosperity
- ❖ lavender oil to de-stress
- ❖ rosemary oil to promote healing
- ❖ bergamot oil to energize yourself

A CALM DEMEANOR

Try to avoid outrage, whether online or in conversation. Outrage, conflict and anger cause your aura to weaken. Dr Andrew Weil, a practitioner of integrative medicine, suggested in one of his early books on optimum health that everyone take regular "news fasts" so we don't take on negativity. This is even more useful for social media. If you don't know what the latest outrage is, you can't fall prey to its effects. Anger and counter-anger can be a very destructive cycle, and nobody—unless they have an abnormal energy exchange that I would not consider beneficial or helpful—feels better after an argument.

WALK BAREFOOT

Connecting with the earth heals you both physically and psychically. If you can manage it, regularly walk barefoot on the earth. This is a process called "earthing," and it ensures that your body clock is calibrated to the pulse of the Earth. It connects you with your own nature and relieves you from the stress of electromagnetic waves that constantly affect our auras.

MEDITATION

In chapter six (pages 124–155) you can find a range of different meditations that you can do to work with your aura and that of others. However, a regular meditation practice, even if you're not trying to do anything in particular, is extremely beneficial. There are now several apps that can help you take a little time each day to relax. You can also take a class if you think it's too difficult to learn to meditate by yourself. Even a few moments relaxing and trying not to think about anything in particular can help you during a busy day.

Seeing the aura

Semyon Davidovich Kirlian invented Kirlian photography in 1939, a process by which he was able to photograph the aura around living things. In 1961, Kirlian and his journalist wife, Valentina, published an article on the subject in the *Russian Journal of Scientific and Applied*

Photography. Ever since that time, researchers and energy healers have used the information gained through Kirlian photography to diagnose illnesses and predict the preoccupations of the people being photographed.

The colors that appear on the photographs have been interpreted by some as corresponding to the meanings of the seven-chakra energy system (see pages 39–53), and by others as being indicative of certain personality traits and of what concerns the person has at the time of being photographed. Kirlian's work has definitely increased the interest in auras, but there was another earlier practitioner who invented a way for people to see the aura with the naked eye.

KILNER SCREENS

Dr W.J. Kilner wrote in his 1911 book *The Human Atmosphere* about investigations he made into the human aura by virtue of his colored screens. The screens are made of thin glass with dicyanin dyes in alcohol. The operator looks through a dark screen at the light screens for a minute or so, and then looks at the person being read through a pale screen until he or she can see the aura. Regular use of the screens results in the operator eventually being able to see auras without the aid of any apparatus. Much like Magic Eye pictures, popular in student culture in the 1990s, once you have adjusted your eye to perceive the aura, it's hard to go back. A plain black or white background behind the subject is required, but looking at the aura in this way can cause pain in the eyes, so should be undertaken with care.

Theosophist Arthur E. Powell described what the aura, seen in this way, looks like in his book *The Etheric Double*: "The Inner Aura is the densest portion of the aura proper. It is usually more distinctly marked and broader in persons in robust physical health. The Outer Aura commences from the outer edge of the Inner Aura and, unlike the Inner Aura, varies in size considerably. Round the head it extends usually about 2 inches beyond the shoulders: by the sides and body of the trunk, it is a little narrower. It follows closely the contours of the body, being sometimes a little narrower down the lower limbs. Around the arms it corresponds to that encircling the legs, but is generally broader round the hands and frequently projects a long distance from the finger tips."

This last part of the description pertaining to the hands will be important for us later when we look at how to balance our auras through our hands (see pages 88–90).

PSYCHIC SIGHT

Despite these more technical ways to see the aura, the most popular among practitioners remains the gift of psychically viewing the aura. This may not necessarily be a visual impression, and it may be that it is "viewed" through feelings and emotions that the healer gets as they sit across from you, in the influence of your aura. Some may even use the flat of the palm to "feel" the edges of the aura by placing their hand a couple of inches away from the body.

If you would like to develop such a sight, you should take care to ensure that you keep your protective sheath in top condition, as you will only be able to get clear impressions of the auras of others if your own is strong and healthy. Otherwise, you may sense gaps in their aura when it is actually a problem with your own. You can find a variety of ways to cleanse your protective sheath on pages 25–31.

CHAPTER 2

Chakras
and auras

The Chakras

Chakras are energy points within the body that act as whirlpools that help distribute energy (called *prana* in Ayurveda and *chi* in Traditional Chinese Medicine) properly inside the body. A blocked chakra can cause problems in the aspect of life that relates to that particular chakra. So, for example, in the seven-chakra system (see below), the heart chakra relates to relationships, and a blockage here will make it hard to attract and maintain loving relationships. It is important to keep your chakras working well, as this will also have an impact on your aura.

THE SEVEN-CHAKRA SYSTEM

Most people would assume that the colorful seven-chakra system that many yogis are familiar with originates in ancient Indian writings—and indeed the Upanishads (800 BCE – 400 BCE) do mention seven chakras. But there is no mention of colors, and many of the healing modalities used in the West would not be recognized by scholars of ancient Indian scriptures. Our modern understanding of the seven-chakra system actually owes more to writers in the 1970s in the West than to the Vedic writings. Since that time, practitioners around the world have accepted the colors given at that time for the seven chakras. However, the mantras associated with them have their root in Vedic writings, where chanting is used to raise energy up the spine from the root to the crown chakra in order to gain spiritual advancement.

MULADHARA
THE ROOT CHAKRA

❖ **Color:** Red
❖ **Mantra:** Laam

The location of this chakra is at the base of the spine, at the point of your pelvic floor. This energy point relates to our basic needs, such as food, shelter, sleep and safety. It is the foundation upon which we are built. If you have weakness or problems in your energy at this chakra, you will find it difficult to trust people and will suffer from a lack of security in your life. You may have nightmares or problems with your lower limbs, and it can result in prostate issues in men. Loss of smell and eating disorders are also indications of problems here.

Interestingly, it used to be rare to find Muladhara problems in people in the developing world. This is counterintuitive, as you would think parts of the world where life is precarious and one's basic needs may not be met would have more root-chakra issues. However, a clue may be found in the fact that traditionally people were far more likely to squat, sitting on the floor rather than on a chair. Even now, one of the ways in which we can bring this chakra back

into alignment is to squat more, whether in *Malasana* (squatting) yogic poses or simply sitting in a squat when at rest.

If squatting is difficult or indeed impossible for you, you can also help balance this chakra through chanting. The mantra for this chakra is laam. The sound is almost "laarm," but as you begin to chant it, you will begin to settle into the sound in a way that feels right to you.

Before you undertake any chakra-clearing work, remember to bathe and put a specific time aside each week to do your chanting. You are trying to impress upon your subconscious that you are about to undertake energetic work.

If you have fears around money and how you will be provided for in the future, returning this chakra to optimum operation will help you let go of those worries. You will find that this first chakra is where you awaken your energy, and it will begin your journey to energetic health. Oddly enough, many strange and wonderful coincidences and events begin to manifest when you begin the work of awakening the kundalini energy that lives here, at the base of your spine. It is very powerful work and should be undertaken by everyone who wishes to live the very best life possible physically, mentally, emotionally and spiritually.

SVADHISTHANA
THE SACRAL CHAKRA

- ❖ **Color:** Orange
- ❖ **Mantra:** Vaam

The location of this chakra is just above the pubic bone and below the navel. Its position is appropriate, as it relates to sexuality as well as creativity. Creativity used to mean the very literal act of creating a child, but in the modern world, this can be about creating a work of art, a home you love, or a relationship that is nurturing and special. You can define what it is that you create.

An imbalance here can result in sexual dysfunction, frustrated creative endeavors, and becoming humorless and sullen. Instead of fearing failure when embarking on any creative endeavor such as painting a picture or learning a dance, embrace it as a natural and enjoyable part of the experience. Laugh if you feel you haven't achieved what you want to because, in truth, all of life is simply play, with an illusion of importance or reality superimposed upon it.

You can do left-nostril breathing as a way to balance this chakra. Close your right nostril with the index and middle fingers of your right hand

and breathe gently 10 times through your left nostril. This increases the feminine energy in your body and is congruent with this chakra's energy makeup. If you feel you have the symptoms of a second-chakra problem, you can do this for seven days before returning to your usual morning breathing practice. Do not do it in conjunction with the alternate-nostril breathing we explore on pages 72–73.

Chanting is another way to balance the chakras. The mantra for this one is vaam, pronounced "vaarm." If you feel that the last sound is extending some way as you chant it, this is fine. Your body has an intuitive knowledge about which sounds you can produce for your healing, so go with it unless you are chanting in a guided group. Chanting in groups is quite different from chanting alone, as you are blending your aura with the auras of everyone else in your group and you must try not to introduce a discordant element into the group chant.

Remember, as always, to instigate a sense of ritual when you sit to chant or do any energy work. Your subconscious must be impressed with the idea that this is a special time in order to properly effect an energetic shift. You can inject your work with ritual by ensuring you do your practices at a particular time of day, in a specific room, or wearing a specific outfit just for energy work. Peace silk (silk extracted without killing silk worms) is particularly good for this purpose, but you can wear any natural, ethically sourced clothes when doing energy work. You then subconsciously know it's time for energy work when you put on those clothes and enter that room at that specific time.

MANIPURA
THE SOLAR PLEXUS CHAKRA

❖ **Color:** Yellow
❖ **Mantra:** Raam

This chakra, located at your solar plexus, just above the navel and below the rib cage, is vitally important for the modern world. That's because this is where the intellect lies, and we often sacrifice the spiritual for the intellectual in modern life. This is also the seat of your personal power and your individual will. It is the chakra that will show you if it is imbalanced in directly observable ways. Digestive problems and loss of confidence are just two problems associated with this chakra. Low self-esteem, lack of self-control and anger-management issues are others.

One way you can bring this chakra into balance is through the exercises given relating to the Naaf on pages 67–69. You can also help heal this chakra by doing the Warrior *asana* on pages 80–81.

This is one of the few energy centers that you can work with on a purely intellectual level by writing out your goals and desires in a journal. If you achieve clarity about where you want to go intellectually, you can use chanting and other energetic practices to manifest those goals and reassure your energy body that you have retained your personal power. It is important for the good functioning of this chakra that you ensure you have expressed your individual will through appropriate maturation and a healthy relationship with your parents. If your relationship with your parents is dysfunctional, consider a class in counseling or another healing therapy in order to resolve it.

The chant for this chakra is raam, which is pronounced as it is written. Try and ensure that you engage your diaphragm by placing your hand on your belly and allowing your breath to go out fully with each chant.

You can also resolve any problems here through diet and intermittent fasting. Please always consult a medical professional before undertaking a fast or considering a change in diet, especially if you are on medication. You can discover your body type, or *dosha,* by booking an Ayurvedic session, which will provide advice on what would be most energetically beneficial for you to eat and drink. Even though it is based on different principles and knowledge, Traditional Chinese Medicine also works very well for digestive problems that arise from a blockage in this chakra. TCM shares the view that the food and drinks we consume affect us energetically, and advice is given on how to come back into equilibrium through a change in nutrition.

ANAHATA
THE HEART CHAKRA

❖ **Color:** Green
❖ **Mantra:** yaam

This chakra is located in the middle of the chest, and is where compassion, love and kindness live. It is vitally important for maintaining good relationships, not just romantically, but also with everyone you come into contact with.

An imbalance here will stop you from feeling loved or being able to give love. The unconditional nature of the love you should give is hinted at in the meaning of the Sanskrit word Anahata; it means "unhurt." In relationships, we are often hurt because we see ourselves as separate from the person we love. If we are concerned with being right over being kind, we will never experience true love.

It is said that a mother's love is the only true love; you may have a hard time believing this if you have an unhappy or abusive relationship with your mother, but it alludes to the fact that, when pregnant, a mother is so intrinsically linked to her baby that what she eats, drinks and feels are felt by her baby through her digestive, respiratory, cardiovascular and hormonal systems. What happens to one happens to the other. This is what true love is: an empathy and sharing of experience so deep that you lose yourself in it. If you are to connect with others in a loving manner, this chakra must be functioning well.

The first way to heal this chakra is by showing self-love. Stop the internal criticism and never speak ill of yourself. Your body and spirit hear everything you say, and calling yourself stupid or clumsy or any of the other negative words we might use is extremely harmful. Buy yourself flowers. Light fragrant candles. Woo yourself and eat dinner for one on your best porcelain plates. Self-care must be a priority, because only when you love yourself can you overflow with love for others.

The chant for this chakra is yaam, and can be pronounced "yum." Imagine as you chant that you are sending out love to all beings in the universe. You can visualize this love as a rose-colored, sparkling energy making its way out of your chest, through your mouth, out into the world and infusing everything with light and joy.

Remember to take that feeling of love and healing into the world outside your meditation room. It's all very well to meditate on love and attempt to clear your heart chakra; but if you're not walking the chant in your everyday life, you will remain blocked here. Smile more. Allow people to cut in front of you in line. Treat everyone as if they were a most beloved part of you.

VISUDDHA
THE THROAT CHAKRA

❖ **Color:** Blue
❖ **Mantra:** Haam

This chakra is located just above your collarbone at the base of your throat, and is the communication center. This is the first of the higher spiritual chakras, and it is most in alignment when you're speaking your truth. This means that you have properly and fully expressed what it is that you hold in your heart.

We often say things to please others; we may agree to do more work for the boss when we know we need a break, or say we'd love to see friends when we'd rather stay at home watching movies and eating ice cream. We may tell someone we'll go on a second date out of guilt rather than because we really want to. This way a blocked throat chakra and an unhappy aura lies.

Do you often get a sore throat? Do you regularly lose your voice? These are both signs that your throat chakra is blocked. A simple way to remedy this immediately is to look at your schedule and see what you have coming up. Is there anything you don't want to do, but are doing out of obligation? Cancel it. Obviously, not everything can be dealt with in this way; you may have a funeral you have to attend, or a sibling's wedding. This is not an excuse to jettison every responsibility you have; but you can definitely think more deeply about what you have agreed to do and excise the things you don't want from your life.

Have you ever had an experience where you've agreed to do something you don't want to do, but then you get sick, so you can't do it anyway? This is because your body will kick into action to respond to whatever you tell it on an energetic level, even if your calendar says something different.

To facilitate better communication, you can wear a blue scarf or necktie for a while. However, chanting works best for this chakra, because sound is its power. The chant for this chakra is haam, and it is pronounced "harm." Open your mouth fairly wide when chanting for this chakra, as you are encouraging yourself to speak up.

You will know yourself which areas in your life require you to speak more truthfully. However, this is not to suggest that you be unkind in anything you say. Remember the golden rule, often attributed to the Sufi poet Rumi: "Before you speak, let your words pass through three gates. At the first gate ask yourself, 'Is it true?' At the second gate ask, 'Is it necessary?' At the third gate ask, 'Is it kind?'"

AJNA
THE THIRD EYE CHAKRA

❖ **Color:** Indigo
❖ **Mantra:** Aum

This chakra is located in the middle of the forehead, between the eyebrows, and is the seat of intuition and a connection to divine consciousness. If you are keen to see auras and develop other psychic skills, this energy center must be working well and in proper alignment. Much like the Vijnanamaya kosha (see page 23), any imbalance here will show up as a disconnection from your intuition and sixth sense.

The Child's Pose (see pages 84–85) is a good yoga *asana* to do to help bring this chakra back into alignment. The *asana* is named well, because our intuition is strongest when we are children and, as we grow into adults, for the sake of society we suppress many of our natural abilities. In Child's Pose, you place your forehead gently on the yoga mat and connect with the earth. This is very healing.

When my step-grandchildren were very young, my son-in-law would gently stroke the place of the third eye between their eyebrows until they fell asleep. Try it yourself with a partner and you will find it very soothing. When we are alert in the day, our intuition is working overtime to keep us safe, so this act relaxes us from alert mode into relaxation mode.

The chant for this chakra is aum and it is pronounced "aa–uu–eemm." This is sometimes written as om, but the pronunciation is better as aum. It is a very powerful chant, and a regular practice with this sound will result in the opening of this high spiritual chakra. People report being able to see auras very easily when they are working with this energy center.

You can also help the working of this chakra by anointing it regularly with a suitable oil after you wash your face in the morning. Jasmine is an oil I use for this purpose, but oils from most night-blooming flowers will work just as well. Avoid rose in anointing this part of the body, as its energy is more suited to the opening of the lower chakras.

You may find that this energy center becomes clear without you needing to do any work on it at all, once you have finished working with the koshas, your protective sheath and the lower chakras. The effect of energy work is cumulative, and works from the physical upwards. So a strong, healthy body with good thoughts, emotions and actions will result in good intuition and higher powers of wisdom and insight.

SAHASRARA
THE CROWN CHAKRA

❖ **Color:** Violet
❖ **Mantra:** None—silent contemplation

This chakra is located at the top of your head, and is the point where we connect to universal energy. If any of your lower chakras are blocked, it will be hard for you to feel the full functioning of this chakra and enjoy the fruits of divine guidance.

It is neither necessary nor advisable to concentrate on opening or unblocking this particular chakra, as it is a gift that we all have when our energy body is working well. It is far better to work on clearing all other chakras and aspects of your energy body. Once this is done, you can establish a meditation practice that includes asking for divine guidance.

You do not have to follow a particular religion or spiritual tradition to enjoy a connection with universal energy. We are beings of light, and our intuition, love and wisdom prove that we are more than just the sum of our flesh and bones.

Colors and their meanings

Most chakra systems use color, but be aware that when you begin working with your energy body, the colors you see (or get an impression of, psychically) may not tally with those of established chakra systems. Don't worry too much about what a color is supposed to mean; concentrate more on what something feels like to you.

For example, the color for the crown chakra in the seven-chakra system is violet, while in the Sufi chakra system, it is an iridescent, shining black. Both are valid, as is whatever you see when you begin to do exercises to view the energy body.

The author Joseph Ostrom has speculated that it may well be that human sight and the colors we are able to see has evolved over the years. "There is some evidence that modern human beings see a larger variety of colors than their ancestors. Homer has described the Aegean Sea as being 'wine-dark'—a dark red? In my travel to the Greek Islands, I have spent a lot of time looking at the sea; believe me, it's a very beautiful light blue-green. It is said that Aristotle saw only reds, greens and yellows. Were the Greeks color-blind? It seems unlikely. Those who are usually have difficulty seeing reds, not blues. The perception of blues seems to be a more recent development for human beings." As such, an obsession with what each color means is not as important as what each color "feels like" to us when we look at it.

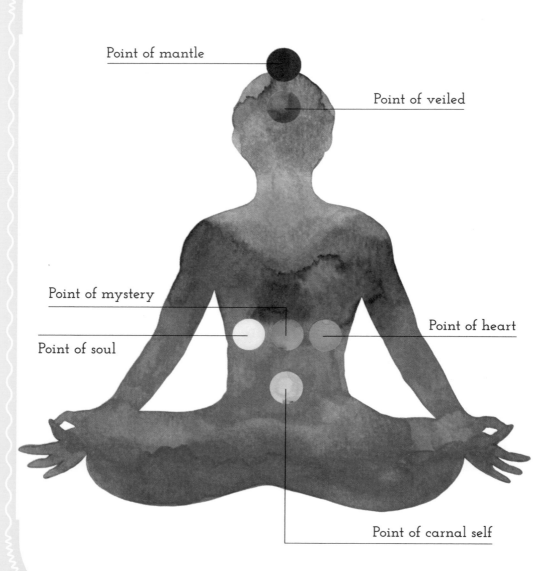

Point of mantle

Point of veiled

Point of mystery

Point of heart

Point of soul

Point of carnal self

The chakras in Sufism

There are six chakras, or *lataif*, in Sufism. The Sufi chakras can be activated through trance dance or *dhikr*, Islamic devotional chanting. Different Sufi traditions attribute different colors and attributes to the energy points in the body. Some only have five points, and there are some who believe that the number of energy centers in the body is infinite since we reflect the universe within ourselves. However, all agree that the *lataif* sit mostly horizontally, across the body, rather than in the vertical formation of the more familiar seven-chakra system. Some Sufi orders do not engage in dance or music, and believe in silent rather than vocal *dhikr*.

All these differences should encourage you because, as you progress through your journey into discovering more about your own aura, you will see what feels most true to you about your energy centers. The most important thing is to trust your intuition. We are somewhat enthralled by facts, figures and science-speak in the West, but energy often uses the ethereal, the intuitive and the mysterious to bring us its best gifts. Stay alert and aware, but also trust yourself if you have a particular sense of your energy.

POINT OF CARNAL SELF

- ❖ **Color:** Yellow
- ❖ **Position:** Its center is in the solar plexus

This is the chakra that pertains to the body and material existence. The body is sacred because it houses your spirit, but in order to fully move forward to the completion of your energetic destiny, you must transcend this *lataifa* (the singular term for chakra).

One of the best ways to do this is to anchor your practice in the body through *dhamal*. *Dhamal* is a Sufi trance dance, and you can obtain drumming tapes that enable you to enter into this state. It is a form of transcendence that shares much with shamanic journeying in that you lose your everyday consciousness in order to commune with the Divine. Initially, you move in rhythm to the beat, but there are no set movements; it is based purely on sensation and how the energy of the drums moves you. It is said that, once in a trance, you become a puppet with strings of energy connecting you to God, and you move whichever way your Maker wants. It is a magical way to clear your first chakra, and you will find that your body may well miraculously heal itself of any number of ailments as a result.

POINT OF HEART

❖ **Color**: Red
❖ **Position**: Its center is an inch or so below the left breast

Sufism is often called the ancient wisdom of the heart, so this point is an important one. It is often through the remembrance of love (and, as we saw when looking at the Anahata chakra on pages 46–47, true love is unconditional) that transcendence is achieved. Ultimate union with the Beloved occurs through the opening of the heart.

Having left the Point of the Carnal Self behind in your energy work, here you begin to meditate on the nature of the Divine and the fact that your soul will return to the source of all creation.

When you are in meditation, you may find that naturally, over time, you feel a warmth in your chest and a sensation of release as this *lataifa* is activated. You will feel an outpouring of love and compassion for all and, ultimately, an understanding of your true nature as a spark of divine energy made manifest for a short time only before returning home to its source.

POINT OF SOUL

❖ **Color:** White
❖ **Position:** Its center is an inch or so below the right breast

The progression of activation of the Sufi chakras is best undertaken with a teacher. For example, chanting is based on the teachings of your tradition, and the correct chant for each *lataifa* is given to the seeker in that setting.

However, it can be revealed that many believe all *lataif* are aspects of the heart, since this is the energy center through which we gain union with the Divine. One of the ways in which you can progress from the dhamal activation of the Point of the Carnal and meditation to open the heart is to undertake gazing at this stage of your journey. There are many ways of gazing and, when you begin to see the auras of people and things, you will become very adept at gazing. Sufis use gazing at one's teacher, or into a mirror, to help unlock the truth in their hearts. You can also do so through *sagale-naseer*, the practice of gazing at the tip of one's nose. This is done when seated in meditation, having done your usual ablutions beforehand.

POINT OF MYSTERY

- ❖ **Color**: Green
- ❖ **Position**: It is situated between the points of heart and soul in the middle of chest

The nature of this *lataifa* is revealed at the correct time for the seeker. Purity is an important concept for all those who would attain the activation of this chakra. We think of purity as simply a function of cleanliness, but this does not just pertain to one's physical body or environment. You can have someone who is physically very clean residing in a tidy, immaculate place, but if they have hate in their heart, the whole energy of the person and place is polluted.

To be pure is to be kind and loving, and to remember the sacred nature of all things since we are all one. We saw earlier that your thoughts matter, so when you feel anger or irritation, stop, breathe and remember to send loving thoughts to whoever has caused you that tension. Only then will the Point of Mystery be open to you and enable you to progress on your journey to enlightenment and union with the Divine.

POINT OF VEILED

- ❖ **Color:** Dark blue
- ❖ **Position:** It is situated in the middle of the forehead, popularly known as the third eye

This is the first of the two higher *lataif,* and is the meeting point between the soul (spirit) and the body. Everything from the Divine comes to this point and is then distributed to other points. This is why whenever you see someone attaining enlightenment in the movies, their third eye is shown as being open or having a light radiating from it.

This chakra will only open and activate once the others are clear and functioning properly. This is because you must be able to handle the energies that come into your body at this stage. Often, problems occur when people are greedy for union with the Divine but they ignore the correct progression of energetic evolution. You wouldn't enter a toddler who didn't yet know how to walk properly into a marathon and expect them to complete it. In much the same way, spiritually you must learn to walk before you can run. Everything happens at the right time, so stay the course and clear your energies in preparation for when enlightenment will find you.

POINT OF MANTLE

❖ **Color**: Shining, iridescent black
❖ **Position**: It is situated in the crown of the head

The mantle is a cloak that envelopes you, and this point is a center of protection. When a parent puts a loving hand on the head of a child, you get the spiritual energy of this *lataifa*. The Divine puts a hand lovingly on our heads at the Point of Mantle. We honor that loving energy by ensuring that we are a worthy recipient of it.

The responsibility we all bear for ourselves culminates at this point. Living with love in our hearts and following good energetic practices will ensure that your energy body is a pure vehicle to be crowned with  this point. However, this second higher *lataifa* does not require any specific practice for its good functioning. Even if we do not activate the other *lataif*, this one is there for the protection of our eternal souls, which are not concerned with the details of our mundane existence. This can be a very cheering thought if you have problems with any of your other chakras, as nobody is ever closed off to the workings of grace.

CHAPTER 3

Balancing
your aura

Physical balance

There is a strong link between your physical body and your aura. Your thoughts affect your physical body and your physical body affects your spiritual one. The three interact constantly, and good health and wellbeing rely on each aspect being well-balanced. It is always a good idea to begin with the physical, as it is the foundation upon which your energetic health is based.

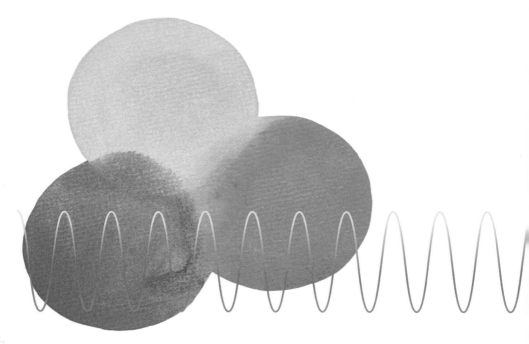

The Naaf

Naaf is a Persian word that means belly button. In the connection between the physical and the spiritual, your belly button is vitally important, and your gut is an organ to which you should pay plenty of attention. The navel is the seat of power in many occult traditions. Swami Brahmavidya wrote in *The Science of Self Knowledge* (1922): "Another great key I will give you is to be found by the contemplation of the Manipur Lotus, which is in the navel, or thereabouts. By contemplating this center, you will be able to enter and go into another person's body, take possession of that person's mind, and cause him to think and to do what you want him to do; you will obtain the power of transmuting metals, of healing the sick and afflicted, and of seership." While no moral modern person wants to take possession of another's mind, healing the sick and obtaining seership would be handy traits to have.

The word "navel" has its root in an old Anglo-Saxon word: *nafela*. The Greek word for navel is *bembix*, which literally means "whirlpool," hinting at how the movement of chakras has been described by almost all energetic medicine practitioners. Most interestingly of all, the root word for "umbilical" in Latin is *umbo*, which means the boss of a shield—the rounded, strongest part of a shield. This is a good indication of how far our strength lies in this part of our bodies.

It is not just the human body that has this center of energy; many believe there are places on Earth that serve the same function in physical geography. In Abrahamic religions, Jerusalem is considered the navel of the world. Cuzco, an important city in Peru, is named for the Quechua (Inca) word for navel. The axis mundi (or center of the Earth) is said to be the place of connection between Heaven and Earth. For the Sioux it is the Black Hills, in the Great Plains of North America. Likewise, Mount Fuji is the axis mundi of Japan. You can read more about places of power on pages 102–106.

NAVEL-GAZING

The term "navel-gazing" is often used in a disparaging way to suggest someone who is far too interested in themselves or in a particular issue to look up and see the bigger picture. However, it actually derives from a spiritual practice common in both ancient Greek and Indian cultures. The Greeks called this *omphaloskepsis*, a contemplation of the navel that was used as an aid to meditation and communion with divinity. Yogis also undertake this practice and activate the Manipura, or solar plexus chakra (see pages 44–45), to gain insight into the nature of the Universe. This chakra center has, in the Western alternative spiritual tradition, been associated with power and purpose. It is considered the seat of will.

You should protect this power center through practical techniques such as rubbing salt over your belly button when having energy-cleansing baths, or wearing a peace silk belt around your waist, under your clothes. Most important of all, keep your gut in good health by following a nutritious diet and paying attention to the foods and drinks that disagree with your digestive system.

Yoga practice

Often there is an assumption that you need to attend classes, buy expensive yoga clothes, mats, blocks and all manner of other equipment in order to practice *asanas*. The truth is that, while yoga classes are useful for ensuring you are doing the postures correctly, you can learn yoga easily. Many people have a daily practice based on watching videos online, while others practice from books. All you really need is comfortable clothing that you can move freely in, and a non-slip, comfortable surface to practice on—this doesn't need to be a yoga mat; you could just use an ordinary rug if it is non-slip. Yoga is always practiced in bare feet.

A morning yoga practice feels very different from an evening one. Begin with 10 minutes each morning and build your practice from that.

Don't practice on a full stomach, and make sure you are sufficiently hydrated. It is good to begin alternate-nostril breathing, as this balances your body and builds a beginning to your *asanas* or postures. On the following pages, there are some simple postures that can help the cleansing of your chakras or the healing of your aura. You can use them as recommended elsewhere for specific problems, or as the core of a regular yoga practice.

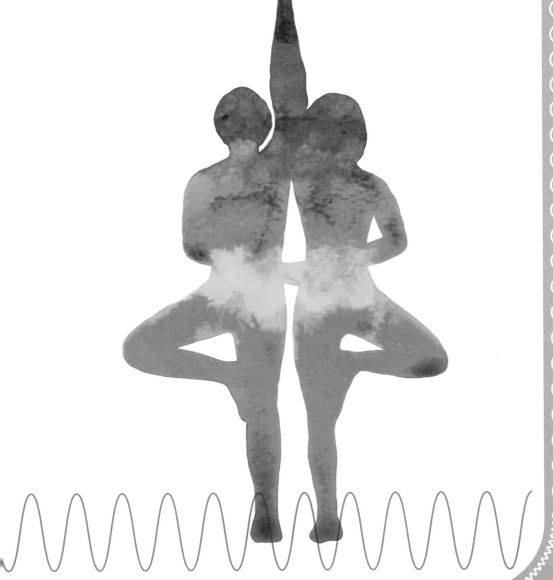

ALTERNATE-NOSTRIL BREATHING

1 Sit cross-legged on the floor, with your back upright. You can use a pillow or cushion to support you if you need it. If you find it hard to sit on the floor, you can sit on a chair. Just be sure to place your feet flat on the ground, hip-width apart.

2 Close your eyes if you feel comfortable doing so. If not, you can leave them shuttered slightly, maintaining a soft gaze.

3 Put your left hand gently on your lap, palm up.

4 Exhale completely and bring the thumb of your right hand up to your right nostril to close it.

5 Inhale through your left nostril and then block it with your little and ring fingers; release your right nostril and exhale out of it.

6 You can rest your index and middle fingers on the third eye.

7 Inhale through the right nostril and close it again with your thumb. Release your left nostril and exhale out of it. This is now one full cycle of alternate-nostril breathing.

8 You can do this for about five minutes or for a number of cycles, but always finish a complete cycle.

This breathing exercise, called *nadi shodhana pranayama,* is a powerful way to balance your energies and focus your mind. It helps with anxiety, lowers stress, and helps your respiratory and cardiovascular systems. It promotes overall wellbeing and is a good daily practice to maintain. However, you should not practice this if you have a cold. And if you have asthma, a lung issue, or any other ailment that affects your breathing, speak to your doctor before you do this exercise.

Prevention, not cure

Y oga is based on the principle that you should prevent illness through a regular practice rather than cure yourself when you are sick. Alla Svirinskaya is a fifth-generation energy healer from Russia who champions sustainable wellness. She says, "It is about wellness as a necessity. Like taking a shower or brushing your teeth. This is a necessity. It is also your necessity to be well. It's not a luxurious aspiration.

"Often, people discover spirituality or go to their doctors or healers when they're at breaking point. Only then, they do something. They're clearing their energy and doing energy rebalancing when they're completely overwhelmed and feel very toxic within. I don't want energy work and energy clearing to be as a desperate SOS kind of measure. What I'm trying to achieve is that people start looking at prophylactics for prevention as part of their daily routine."

Alla makes an excellent point. Ideally, we should not be clearing and balancing our auras once we are already sick; good energetic health should be a daily concern. The following yoga *asanas* will help you prevent energetic illnesses when practiced regularly.

MOUNTAIN POSE

1 Stand with your feet hip-width apart. Ensure your feet are parallel.

2 Root down with the heels and the balls of your feet, spread and extend your toes, and draw up the arches of your feet.

3 Draw your knees and thigh muscles upwards.

4 Press the tops of the inner thighs back and the tailbone forward. Draw the lower abdomen and navel in and up.

5 Lengthen the spine upwards, lift the breastbone, allowing the shoulders to relax back and down; broaden the chest.

6 Lift the crown of the head while pressing the soles of the feet down, particularly the heels and the mounds of the toes, into the ground.

7 Extend your arms down the sides of the body, palms facing your thighs. Gaze straight ahead and breathe steadily. Remain in the pose for 20 seconds.

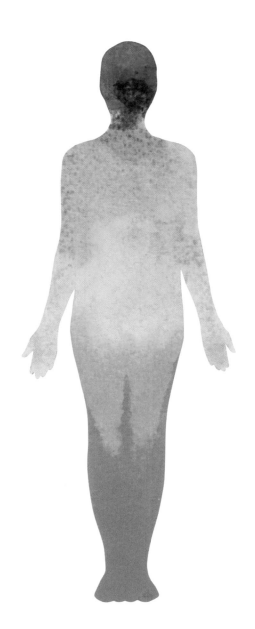

TREE POSE

1 Stand in mountain pose (see page 76).

2 Put your weight on your left foot; raise your right leg and bend it at the knee. Place your raised foot on the inner thigh or the inner shin of your left leg. (Avoid placing the foot on the inner knee.) Your toes should be pointing downwards.

3 Join your palms together above your head. If this feels too difficult, you can bring your hands down into prayer position in front of you.

4 If you feel unstable, place a hand on the wall for support.

5 Let your spine lengthen upwards as you press the foot of your standing leg firmly down.

6 Feel the sense of being grounded as you root down.

7 Gaze straight ahead at eye level. This will help you balance.

8 Stay as long as feels comfortable; return to mountain pose.

9 Repeat on the other side.

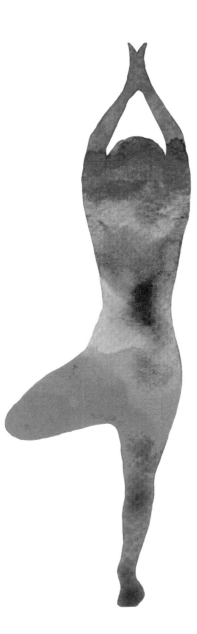

WARRIOR POSE

1   Stand in mountain pose (see page 76).

2   Turn to the side of your mat and extend your feet approximately 3-4 feet apart.

3   Raise your arms above your head, palms facing each other. Yours arms should be straight and shoulder-width apart. (If your shoulders are tight or uncomfortable, take your arms wider apart.)

4   Turn your right foot 90 degrees to the right, and turn your back foot in to the right.

5   Bend your right knee. Your right knee should be positioned over your right heel, not collapsing inwards and not going beyond the heel.

6   Press down on your left outer heel; press your inner left thigh back; take your tailbone forwards. Stretch your body upwards. Gaze straight ahead.

7   Hold for 15-20 seconds, then come up out of the pose. Repeat on the other side.

COBRA POSE

1 Lie prone (front-side down) on the floor.

2 Stretch your legs back and press the front of your thighs and feet into the ground. Draw your tailbone to the ground.

3 Place your hands flat on the floor by the sides of your chest with your elbows hugging the sides of your body.

4 On an inhalation, start to lift your chest off the ground by pressing your hands firmly down and starting to straighten the arms.

5 Draw the navel up toward the chest, drop the shoulders down away from the ears, lift the sternum without the front ribs flaring.

6 Ensure the backbend is evenly distributed throughout the spine to avoid putting pressure on the lower back.

7 Do not strain the back by trying to come up too high. Keeping the elbows bent rather than straightening the arms completely will help avoid potential strain.

8 Stay in the pose for up to 30 seconds; then, on an exhalation, lower your body down and rest.

CHILD'S POSE

1 Kneel down on all fours.

2 Your knees should be slightly more than hip-width apart. Bring your big toes together. Move your sitting bones back to rest on your heels. You can place a rolled-up blanket or towel under your feet if there is discomfort in the front of the feet, and/or, similarly, between the backs of your thighs and your calves if your sitting bones don't reach your heels.

3   On an exhalation, bend forward from the hips, keeping the front of your body long, and rest your torso between your thighs.

4   Place your forehead on the ground, or, if it does not reach the ground, rest your forehead on a block (or book). Your head should not hang without support. Observe the place where your forehead meets the ground or support.

5   Extend your arms out in front of you, palms face-down.

6   This is a resting pose—there should be no discomfort in your knees, legs, shoulders or back. Let your breath be easy and fluid.

7   Rest in this position for up to 2 minutes.

8   Exit the pose on an inhalation, pressing your hands into the floor to lift up your body.

CORPSE POSE

This is the ultimate pose for balancing all your energy centers and bringing yourself back into alignment. It is a good *asana* to finish your practice on.

1   Sit on the floor and extend your legs out in front of you. Then slowly lower yourself to the ground until you are lying supine on the floor.

2   Let your arms and legs fall away from the sides of your body. Turn your palms to face the ceiling, and let your legs and feet relax out to the sides. Ensure your limbs are as symmetrical as possible to enable optimal relaxation.

3 Place a pillow under your knees if there is any tension in your back; alternatively, you can support the lower legs on the seat of a chair.

4 Place a folded blanket under your head and neck if your head is tilted backwards.

5 Close your eyes and allow your body to relax; surrender the weight of the body to the ground beneath you.

6 Keep your attention on your breathing, and try to remain completely still.

7 Stay in the pose for up to 5 minutes, then slowly bring your awareness back, open your eyes, draw your knees up and over to the right and then push yourself up to a seated position.

Hand healing

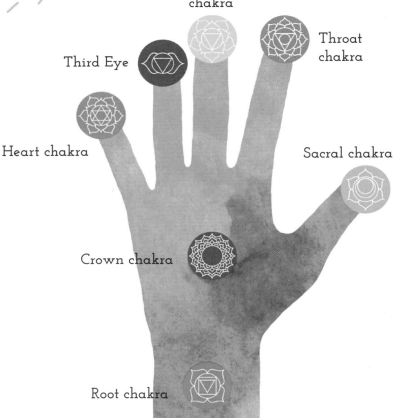

Solar plexus
chakra

Throat
chakra

Third Eye

Heart chakra

Sacral chakra

Crown chakra

Root chakra

One of the best ways you can balance your aura is through your hands. The aura is denser here, so your hands should be more naturally protected than other parts of your body. Hands are also connected to all the organs and energy points in your body, so manipulating your hands can help you heal that part of your body and your life.

However, you can also impart healing through hands-on touch. We have already seen the beneficial effects of massage, but once you are able to view the aura, you will also be able to direct energy through your hands to balance and heal the other person's aura.

You can visualize opening your hands' chakras by shaking them gently in front of you with the palms facing toward you. You can also do so by rubbing your hands vigorously together until they feel warm and tingly. That sensation is an indication that you have activated the chakras of your hands and can apply them to draw energy from the universal source into whoever you are healing.

HENNA CIRCLES

A simple henna design, such as the one shown, is often used in the subcontinent to cool the hands (and consequently the hand chakras) as well as to attract prosperity and good luck to the wearer. Henna is a natural dye that has been used around the world in rites and rituals.

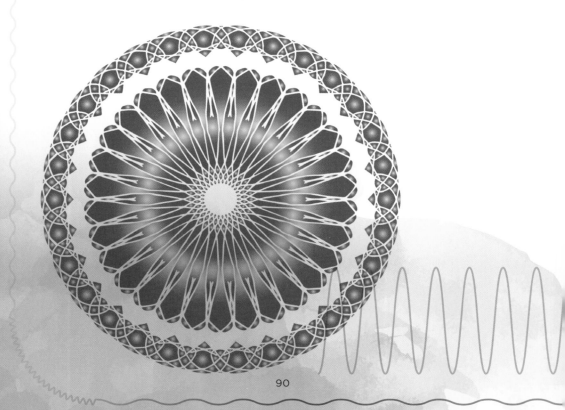

ENERGY SPHERE

One of the ways you can both sense and balance your aura is to do the following exercise.

1 Sit in a straight-backed chair with your feet flat on the floor.

2 Hold your hands out in front of you with the palms facing inwards.

3 Draw your hands in until they are an inch apart, but not touching.

4 Feel the sensation of resistance between your palms. This is your aura's energy that you're feeling.

5 Move your hands apart and together again until you get a clearer sensation of the energy between them.

6 You can then visualize that energy forming a sphere that you are holding in your hands like a ball.

7 Within that ball of light, visualize your entire body with a strong, healthy aura around it.

8 Finally, send that energetic sphere up to the heavens above your head.

CHAPTER 4

The environment
and other people

Your sacred space

Have you ever been in the midst of a city crowd? Most of us feel very uncomfortable in such a situation. This is because there are several auras chaotically assaulting the borders of our own aura. On occasion, if your own aura is weak, you will attract people and situations that cause irritation and frustration in daily life. A delayed train. An impatient commuter shoving you out of the way. Spilt coffee.

The way to prevent this from happening is to ensure that you are recharging somewhere that is completely in alignment with your energy body. Your home may not currently be a sacred space in the way that a church or temple might be, but you should aim to get it there. You can create a sacred space more or less anywhere, but there are certain things you should do when you're first starting to clear your space.

DECLUTTER AND DETOX

While it's fine to have a lot of possessions or collections, clutter is not good for your aura or the auras of the people and animals that live in your home. Clutter can be defined as something you don't need and don't love. People often harm their auras by not handling their clutter. This is because clutter essentially represents decisions that haven't been made. So every time you see that stack of papers that hasn't been filed, or that pile of clothes that hasn't been donated or washed, you feel guilt. Guilt is toxic to your aura. Prolonged guilt will damage your aura, so you must address it as soon as possible.

Having cleared your clutter (and get help if you find it too stressful to deal with by yourself), you should give everything in your home a spring clean. Do not use harsh chemicals, as they inevitably hurt both your physical body and your auric one. There are many natural ingredients, including baking soda, lemon and vinegar, that are good for cleaning; also, there are plenty of health-food stores that stock natural, chemical-free household cleaners.

Once this is done, you'll find that the energy has shifted somewhat in your home. At this point, you can dedicate it to your highest good by smudging (see pages 25–26) and stating your intention to create a nourishing, safe and happy home.

Then, walk from your front door clockwise around each room in your house, holding your hands out in front of you. Try to sense the energy of your furniture, possessions, décor and layout. Does anything feel a bit "sticky," or as if it's in the wrong place? Now is a good time to rearrange furniture or thin out artwork if it doesn't feel right.

COLORS AND THEMES

Blues are among the most calming and aura-friendly colors to have in your home. White is also very soothing. However, do not reject reds and oranges automatically, as a deep red bedroom can be reminiscent of the womb and can therefore feel very safe and cozy. Orange is also great for kitchens, as it stimulates the appetite and aids digestion.

Choose patterns, motifs and themes with care, as each has meaning and consequences for how you will feel in your space. Generally, materials such as wood and textiles are better for the human aura than metal and plastic, so try to make sure that pieces of furniture, such as your bed, are made of wood.

Share your space with plants and animals, if you can. Ferns and spider plants are great air purifiers, and have calming auras that will ensure the overall atmosphere in your house remains clean and uplifting.

Pets are excellent at reading auras, and will naturally gravitate toward those whose auras indicate that they are friendly and good. They also sense when you need a cuddle due to emotional distress, and will attempt to cheer you up without prompting.

DIGITAL DETOX

It is not practical to recommend that you do away with all digital devices, since most of our lives are now lived on apps and mobile phones. However, you should put away your phone when doing two vital things: sleeping and eating. The electromagnetism that mobile phones emit when in use affect our auras badly. It is simple enough to leave your phone charging in a different room when you go to bed. You should also put down the phone and turn off the TV when you're eating. You can help this process by having a dining table or a dedicated place where you sit to eat. Make meals sacrosanct, and always give your full attention to the process of nourishing your body.

When items like TVs, computers and stereos are not in use, turn them off at the socket rather than leaving them on sleep. This is to ensure that any electromagnetic frequencies are kept to a minimum in your home. If you want to get really radical in the pursuit of a clear aura, consider not having a TV at all. I know a number of very happy people who don't have one.

Places of power

There are some people who return again and again to the same vacation destination each year. They visit the same bars and restaurants, see the same sights, and enjoy the same activities at around the same time each year. You may consider them unadventurous, but actually they are very fortunate for, generally speaking, these are people who have found the aura of a place that agrees with their own personal energy makeup.

If you manage to find a place that attracts you and makes you feel great, it may well be your own personal place of power. You feel invigorated there; your shoulders relax, as does your jaw, and you feel as though you have been transported to a delightful place.

FINDING YOUR PLACE IN THE WORLD

There are some obvious contenders for finding a place to give you solace. Stone circles have traditionally been centers of energy and ritual for Pagan and Neolithic communities in Britain and Ireland. These are powerful, not just because of where they're located (usually built along energetic lines that are particularly potent), but also because the aura of a place is influenced by its history. Where sacred rituals and rites have taken place, the area takes on an aura of power and transcendence that is almost magical. This is, on occasion, ruined by human beings when they commodify the experience and turn it into a gimmick or a novelty, but you can still find amazing places off the beaten track that align to the cravings of our auras.

Stone circles have fascinating auras that join to create a shield around the whole area.

Water is another attraction for the human aura. Oceanfront and riverside properties always cost more money because of the truism that we are attracted to water. Moving water will keep the energy of a place clear and light, while stagnant water in ponds or manmade lakes can exude melancholy due to the lack of connection with the world's water system.

However, not all manmade structures suffer from this problem. Wells and portals or holes made in stone act as energy points from which you

The Sufi monastery of Blagaj Tekke in Blagaj, Bosnia, is built next to the source of the river Buna. Rivers and moving water are classic ways to tap into the energy of the Earth.

Wells and stone portals act like the chakras of the Earth, allowing energy to pool and move outward into the world.

can draw energy into the world. In myth and legend, we often hear of these holes, and know to fear and respect their power. Passing through a stone circle almost always leads you to the fairy world, so these gateways have a touch of the magical to them.

If you find a place of power that resonates with you, but you are unable to visit it as often as you like, you can connect with it using the meditation on pages 146–149. This is a great way to enhance your auric connection to the area, and you may find that opportunities begin to open up that will lead you to being able to visit it in real life soon.

If you find that you are living in a part of the world that doesn't agree with you or your aura, you will never be able to find happiness until you leave, so you must work to bring about that change. This can't be done by criticizing or denigrating the place where you live. It can only be done by praising the place where you think you will be happier. Attraction rather than rejection must be your operating procedure.

Helping others

H ealing your friends and family is an act that not only helps them, but also helps you. This is because if you could see your aura, you would see tendrils of energy stretching out and connecting you with everyone you know. Some tendrils, for example those connecting you to your life partner, are like thick cords that connect you strongly to another person's energy. Others, like those connecting you to the cashier at your local supermarket, are faint but nevertheless present. Whenever we think about someone, a tendril zooms out and connects with their energy. It doesn't matter how physically far away that person is—the tendril will still find them. Some religions believe that when you pray for your dead, the prayer energy reaches the person in heaven and gives them both pleasure and merit.

TEA AND SYMPATHY

While not every person you love will want to explore the world of auras with you, you can help heal their aura by doing something quite mundane. Sharing tea with someone is an easy way to connect with their energy, give them some of your healing vibes, and make them feel loved.

These teas are particularly good for the aura:
- ❖ Chamomile
- ❖ Rosehip
- ❖ Nettle
- ❖ Peppermint
- ❖ Jasmine

AFFIRMATIONS

If you have a friend who is a little more open-minded about auric healing, you can try partnered affirmations. An affirmation is a positive, present-timed statement of what you would like to manifest in your life. When you say them aloud with a friend who repeats them back to you, it creates an auric bond that makes the outcome far more likely. This is because there is

someone else witnessing your affirmation and confirming it back to you.

So you might say, "I am strong and healthy." Then your friend says to you, "You are strong and healthy."

Or you might do an affirmation to manifest wealth or a loving relationship. What you choose to affirm is up to you, but the statement must be in the present tense, so no "I will be…". And it must be positive, so no statements that begin "I am not…"

After you say your affirmations to each other and repeat them back to each other, make a note of what you said and the date when you said it; then look back once your outcomes have manifested. Did anything not manifest? What do you or your friend believe is blocking that outcome for you both? How can you convince yourself?

For example, suppose you affirmed "I am fit enough to run a marathon," but you didn't manage to run one despite your friend affirming it back to you. It may be that you are fit enough to run a marathon, but you didn't affirm that you have successfully completed a marathon. Or it may be that you have done nothing beyond the affirmation to meet your goal. The affirmation will help, but you still need to put in the training sessions. Reaffirm your goal and report back to your friend each time you undertake a training session so that your friend is also convinced that your goal will be met.

Interestingly, Alla Svirinskaya, the hugely talented Russian medical doctor and healer mentioned earlier, has discovered that it is best to say affirmations in the language you used from when you learned to talk until around the age of 10. For me this is Punjabi and, in learning this nugget of useful information, I found my affirmations moved up a level as a result of saying them in Punjabi.

ABSENCE OF AN AURA

In your early days of trying to see auras, you may find that you do not see anything at all—and that is absolutely fine. However, some say that the absence of an aura can be a sign of impending death. The famous psychic Edgar Cayce wrote of a very sad and dramatic experience in his pamphlet *Auras*. He had been shopping in a department store and was going to take the elevator. As the doors opened, he felt a dark hollowness inside it, despite it being quite full of people. At that exact moment, a red sweater caught his eye, and he motioned for the elevator to leave without him, intending to catch the next one. The cable snapped on the elevator and all the occupants plunged to their deaths. Cayce wrote how odd the whole experience had been, since he didn't even like the color red. Thankfully, in our explorations of auras, not seeing an aura will not mean anything other than that we need a lot more practice.

CHAPTER 5

Energetic
protection

Vital energy

You should appreciate that your aura is ever-changing and your energy body is forever moving and leaping with your changing emotions, thoughts and behaviors. However, your aura needs regular replenishment with vital energy. A healthy person replenishes their energy through exercise, being in nature, and engaging in activities that elevate their consciousness. An unhealthy person drains their energy and causes damage to their aura through overwork, bad diet, and engaging in criticism of both themselves and others.

I have never watched drama-infused TV shows because I feel that they harm the psyche. The louder and more aggressive a program is, the more you will attract that sort of behavior into your life, because your aura begins to reorder itself into the shape of the damaged aura of someone who has a lot of drama and conflict in their life.

You can draw lots of healing energy from nature due to its superabundant ability to replenish auras.

Energy Vampirism

It is not just a diet of bad TV and overwork that damages your aura. On occasion, illness, trauma or certain psychic practices can cause "wounds" in the aura where energy leaks out and depletes a person's vital life force. This can cause them to, quite unconsciously, seek energy sources that are not appropriate. Chiefly, this means draining others of their vital energy. When you are with such people, you may find that you feel exhausted and low afterwards, while they go away feeling refreshed and replenished. This is because the energy drain has left you depleted while they have been topped up with your vital force.

What can you do about this? Don't, whatever you do, accuse your friend or acquaintance of being an energy vampire! Nobody will respond well to such an accusation, and the vast majority of people have no idea that they're doing this. Your best bet is to keep your time with them to a minimum and make your way to a place of natural beauty soon after you have seen them, as trees are natural super-producers of vital energy, and taking some of that vital force from them will harm neither the trees nor yourself.

You can even be drained of energy on the phone or a video call. The person does not need to be in the room with you to drain your energy. This is a characteristic of the fact that energy does not follow the rules of physical engagement, but is on a different, more mobile plane.

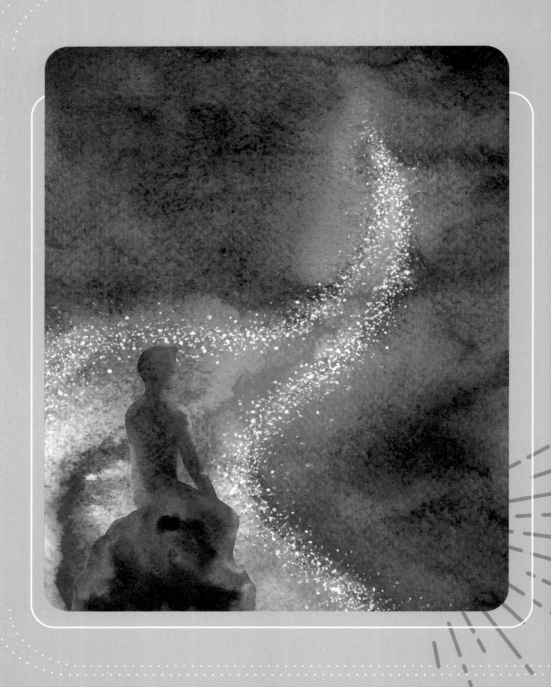

Cord-cutting

If you find that you continue to feel depleted by a particular person and, after seeing them, no amount of time with trees is helping, you can choose to do a cord-cutting. As we saw earlier, every time we think of someone, a tendril of light energy connects us to them. Often if we begin to dread seeing someone, those tendrils become stronger, as we are still thinking about them—even if negatively.

If you are ready to have that person leave your life entirely—for example, in the case of an abusive ex—then you can do a cord-cutting. This is where you cut the energetic ties connecting you to a person and it results in a real-life break from them. Sit in meditation in the way that the meditations chapter teaches (pages 124–155) and think about the person. Then imagine the new tendril connecting you to that person. This will enable you to view the cord that is tying you to them. Imagine a white light sword in your mind's eye, and have it swiftly and cleanly cut through the cord. Imagine that your end of the cord retreats back into your whole and healed aura. You do not have to visualize it, but you can rest assured that their end of the cord has also retreated to their own energy body.

Once this is done, make a conscious effort to avoid thinking about, communicating or talking about the person. You have now moved on energetically and physically.

Thought-forms

The pineal gland is what enables thoughts to reach out into the world and manifest. It is used extensively in clairvoyance. Our auras can retain both positive and negative thought-forms within them, sometimes manifesting to those with psychic sight as symbols in the aura. Negative thought-forms can cause many problems in the physical world, as they are the result of painful or unhelpful beliefs. If you were told that you were stupid as a child, that thought-form can get trapped in your aura and needs to be released if you are to regain your psychic protection. You can release this form through an affirmation, an auric healing with a practitioner, or through a period of meditation.

You can then replace negative thought-forms with strong, positive ones. If you can create an impression in your mind of an outcome that is desirable to you, and put enough passion behind it, it will arise as a thought-form that must manifest in real life.

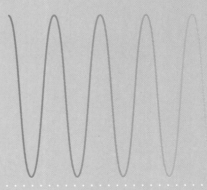

Attracting the wrong people

Before she met her husband, my eldest daughter attracted the strangest, most arrogant, difficult men in the northern hemisphere. One evening she brought home another terrible date who was rude and dismissive. So, naturally, I scolded her. Now, before you worry that I am an awful father, my children have been brought up to understand energy. They know that if they are attracting things that are wrong for them, there is definitely something happening there energetically that is not just bad luck.

"Why do you think that this is the sort of person you deserve in a relationship?" I asked her.

When we drilled down into the truth of it, it appeared that she had an erroneous belief that she wasn't attractive enough to get the best men to date her. When I asked her how and when she had started believing this thoroughly incorrect thought, she realized that it was a lie she had been telling herself since her teenage years. She released it, and her wonderful husband came into her life very quickly and very easily. In much the same way, when you release the wrong, negative thought-forms from your aura, you will attract what is best for you.

Intuitive scanning

You should get into the habit of intuitively scanning situations before you enter them. If you get to the stage where you can see auras quite clearly, you will find that you can just soften your eyes and see the information you need from a scenario—for example, whether to get the oncoming train or the one after it.

You may find that you can't visually see anything and, in such a case, you should develop your intuition to give you the same helpful information. If you are faced with two paths, you can, at the point of choice, "feel" which is the best one for you. Ensuring you are regularly engaging in the cleansing practices on pages 25–31 will help you develop that intuitive sense.

CHAPTER 6

The meditations

Meditation to see your own aura

D o not be discouraged if, the first time you do this meditation, you are unable to see your aura. It is said that it takes at least 42 days of daily meditation before you can fully see changes in energy—so a regular practice is vitally important.

1 Ensure that you are in a calm mood. Sip water. Breathe in and out in a gentle, conscious, yet unforced way.

2 Once you have reached a feeling of calm, close your eyes and state your intention to see your energy body.

3 Keeping your eyes closed, place your hands, one over the other, at your belly button with the palm of the hand closest to your body resting gently on your stomach.

4 As you breathe in and out, imagine that there is a force field of light that is emanating from your body on the in breath and contracting toward your body on the out breath. This may seem counterintuitive, but energy follows the physical body and, as you breathe out, your lungs deflate and your chest cavity gets smaller, thereby bringing your energy body closer to your physical body.

5 In your imagination, start at the top of your head and "scan" down your body, looking for any areas where the energy feels different. Is there stagnation around your shoulder blades? Does your energy feel fragmented around an old injury? Keep going until you reach the soles of your feet.

6 Now open your eyes, and hold your hands out in front of you with the palms facing toward you. If you are wearing a ring,

leave it on, and look at the dividing space between the ring and your finger. Soften your eyes and see if you can see a blurring at the edges of your hands. Do you get any impression of color or shapes, lines or textures here?

7 After a few minutes, rub your palms together, close your eyes and place your hands over your eyes to soothe them.

8 Record your impressions of what you saw or thought about during the meditation in a journal. Do this for at least a month, and look back to see if any insights about your energy have emerged.

TIPS

❖ Ensure you practice your meditation at the same time each day.

❖ Try and sit on an upright chair with your feet flat on the ground and your back supported by the back of the chair.

❖ Ideally, sit in front of a white or light-colored wall. If this is not possible, ensure there is no visual clutter in front of you.

Meditation to see the auras of others

Seeing the auras of others will help you understand them better and feel more compassion for them. However, it is best to practice this meditation alone and then try to see a friend's aura first before trying with strangers. The sort of "seeing" this requires will make it look like you are staring at or beyond people and, in some cultures, this can be considered rude—so be aware of how you practice this skill.

1 Ensure that you are in a calm mood. Sip water. Breathe in and out in a gentle, conscious, yet unforced way.

2 Once you have reached a feeling of calm, close your eyes and state your intention to be able to see the auras of others.

3 Keeping your eyes closed, place your hands, one over the other, at your belly button with the palm of the hand closest to your body resting gently on your stomach.

4 As you breathe in and out, imagine that there is a force field of light that is emanating from your body on the in breath and

contracting toward your body on the out breath. Then rest your hands, palms up, on your lap.

5 In your imagination, see a tower of light entering into the top of your head. This is a white sparkling column of light and, as you gaze with your mind's eye, you can see that the column goes up into a web or net high above you. That web has many, many columns of light connecting to other people all over the world. You cannot see above the web of light, but you can see that it connects all people together.

6 Look down the column of light to the person nearest to you (you may find that you get the impression of it being a friend or close relation, or someone you live with). Imagine there is a sheath of light around their body. What does it look like? Is it clear? Any colors, gaps or breaks in their energy body? Where are those gaps?

7 Thank them for allowing you to observe their energy, and give them a blessing for their highest good (even if this is a person you do not get along with in daily life).

8 Turn your palms downward on your lap and rub them against your thighs. Gently open your eyes when you are ready.

AFTER THE MEDITATION

Ask a friend if you can try and look at their aura. It may even be the person you saw in your meditation, but it doesn't have to be. Seat them in front of a light-colored wall, or at least a clutter-free background. Soften your eyes and "scan" their body from top to bottom. Look for colors, movement in the energy, gaps or filaments of light. Do not attempt to interpret what any of this means, and don't panic your friend by saying you can see gaps in their energy! Ask questions about any parts you see unusual energy around, just to see if you're picking up on anything they may have experienced. For example, if you see a grayish color around their knees, ask them how their knees are. You may find they have arthritis or knee pain. Over time, you will be able to check over anyone's aura just by adjusting how you look at them.

Meditation to connect with your houseplants

Sometimes we have a houseplant that, no matter what we do, seems determined to die. It may be that it is energetically not for us, and we may be better off giving it to someone who it might thrive with. However, if you want to connect with your plants in a more meaningful way, you can also try this meditation. You do not need to have the ailing plant in front of you, but it may help your visualization if it is in the same room.

1   Ensure that you are in a calm mood. Sip water. Breathe in and out in a gentle, conscious, yet unforced way.

2   Once you have reached a feeling of calm, close your eyes and state your intention to energetically connect with your plants.

3   Keeping your eyes closed, place your hands, one over the other, at your belly button with the palm of the hand closest to your body resting gently on your stomach.

4   As you breathe in and out, imagine that there is a force field of light that is emanating from your body on the in breath and contracting toward your body on the out breath. Then rest your hands, palms up, on your lap.

5   In your mind's eye, visualize a leaf. It can be the shape of a leaf of the plant you wish to connect with or it can be a generic leaf to represent all plants. The only important thing is that you see it clearly in your mind's eye.

6   See a light emanating from the leaf, causing it to glow from within. Note any colors or filaments and any impressions that occur about the energy of plants.

7   Thank the "spirit of plants," for that is what you've been connecting with, for allowing you to observe its energy and give a blessing to all plants, especially those living in your home. You can also concentrate on sending healing thoughts to any plant in your home that is particularly unwell.

8   Turn your palms downward on your lap and rub them against your thighs. Gently open your eyes when you are ready.

Meditation to see through the eyes of an animal

Many animals see things radically differently from humans. For example, bees can see ultraviolet light that humans can't see. Scent can almost be "seen" by dogs and cats since it is so pronounced and is a marker for territory. Birds can see the Earth's magnetic field. It can be good to sometimes "see" through the eyes of an animal, as it gives you another perspective into the invisible energies that are all around us.

1   Ensure that you are in a calm mood. Sip water. Breathe in and out in a gentle, conscious, yet unforced way.

2   Once you have reached a feeling of calm, close your eyes and state your intention to be able to see through the eyes of an animal.

3   Keeping your eyes closed, place your hands, one over the other, at your belly button with the palm of the hand closest to your body resting gently on your stomach.

4 As you breathe in and out, imagine that there is a force field of light that is emanating from your body on the in breath and contracting toward your body on the out breath. Then rest your hands, palms up, on your lap.

5 Think of the animal whose eyes you'd like to see through. It is better if you pick a wild animal that is representative of all of its species and is not in your life. It is a bad idea to pick a pet, as your pets already have an energetic link to you and may not like the sensation of you connecting with them in that way.

6 Visualize how that animal sounds, looks, moves and eats. Imagine it doing a normal everyday action such as eating, and then imagine that you're seeing the food it's eating because you are looking out from its eyes. Is it a predator or prey animal? Do you see what is in front of you or to the sides? Can you see colors? Lines of energy?

7 Once you have noted your impressions, thank the animal for permitting you to look out of its eyes for a while, and send blessings to all animals.

8 Turn your palms downward on your lap and rub them against your thighs. Gently open your eyes when you are ready.

Meditation to attract loving relationships

This meditation works irrespective of whether you're single, attached, or not interested in romantic relationships at all. It is to attract a loving quality in *all* your relationships including parents, siblings, friends, colleagues and acquaintances. It is likely to find you fostering a friendlier connection even with strangers you meet, including commuters on your train or the person who sells you your monthly travel pass.

1 Ensure that you are in a calm mood. Sip water. Breathe in and out in a gentle, conscious, yet unforced way.

2 Once you have reached a feeling of calm, close your eyes and state your intention to be able to attract and maintain loving relationships.

3 Keeping your eyes closed, place your hands, one over the other, at your belly button with the palm of the hand closest to your body resting gently on your stomach.

4 As you breathe in and out, imagine that there is a force field of

light that is emanating from your body on the in breath and contracting toward your body on the out breath. Then rest your hands, palms up, on your lap.

5　Imagine a column of rose-pink sparkling light coming down from the heavens and entering you at the top of your head.

6　Feel that light filling your body and emerging out of every pore. Feel the love that this light represents, and then imagine it emanating outward to encompass your family, your friends, your community, your country, your continent and your world.

7　Say out loud: "I walk in loving kindness; I speak with loving kindness; I act with loving kindness."

8　Turn your palms downward on your lap and rub them against your thighs. Gently open your eyes when you are ready.

Meditation to attract wealth

L ife can sometimes throw wildcards at you that affect your wealth and wellbeing. In such times, your aura reacts and you find yourself unable to be a good, clear vessel for holding money and prosperity. When this occurs, and you feel abundance slipping away, it is good to do this meditation to switch your aura back into attracting instead of repelling mode.

1   Ensure that you are in a calm mood. Sip water. Breathe in and out in a gentle, conscious, yet unforced way.

2   Once you have reached a feeling of calm, close your eyes and state your intention to be able to attract and maintain loving relationships.

3   Keeping your eyes closed, place your hands, one over the other, at your belly button with the palm of the hand closest to your body resting gently on your stomach.

4   As you breathe in and out, imagine that there is a force field of light that is emanating from your body on the in breath and

contracting towards your body on the out breath. Then rest your hands, palms up, on your lap.

5 Imagine a column of green jade-colored, sparkling light coming down from the heavens and entering you at the top of your head.

6 Feel that light filling your body and emerging out of every pore. Feel the prosperity and wealth that this light represents, and then imagine it emanating outward from you, where it magnetizes money and wealth opportunities, and draws them to you.

7 Say out loud: "I release lack; I am abundantly wealthy."

8 Turn your palms downward on your lap and rub them against your thighs. Gently open your eyes when you are ready.

Meditation to heal your environment

We can sometimes feel powerless to affect our environment. We hear and see news that about the climate crisis, we can see plastic pollution in the oceans, and we worry about what the future will hold if our planet's ecosystem is unable to heal from the strain we have put on it. Doing this meditation can help you appreciate that we are all connected to each other and to the planet. Sending healing energy to the environment you live in is a pure endeavor that has benefits for all.

1   Ensure that you are in a calm mood. Sip water. Breathe in and out in a gentle, conscious, yet unforced way.

2   Once you have reached a feeling of calm, close your eyes and state your intention to be able to heal your environment.

3   Keeping your eyes closed, place your hands, one over the other, at your belly button with the palm of the hand closest to your body resting gently on your stomach.

4 As you breathe in and out, imagine that there is a force field of light that is emanating from your body on the in breath and contracting toward your body on the out breath. Then rest your hands, palms up, on your lap.

5 Imagine a column of white light coming down from the heavens and entering you at the top of your head.

6 Feel that light filling your body and emerging out of every pore. As the light pours out of you, it begins to pool under your hands at your belly button. Move your hands to accommodate the pooling energy that begins to form a sphere in front of your stomach.

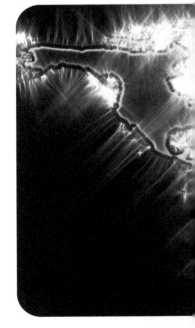

7 Within that ball of light, visualize the outcome that you would like for your environment. You could imagine walking along a pristine beach with no litter and no plastic in the ocean. Or you could imagine an abundant rainforest with the sound of birdsong and forest animals. Closer to home, you could visualize your community coming together to pick up litter or to create a public park or garden.

8 Once you have you created that vision in your ball of light, physically guide the light up over your head and out into the divine dimensions.

9 Feel gratitude for living where you live and for having space in this dimension. Give thanks for all the energies in the spiritual realm who help you every day in your life.

10 Turn your palms downward on your lap and rub them against your thighs. Gently open your eyes when you are ready.

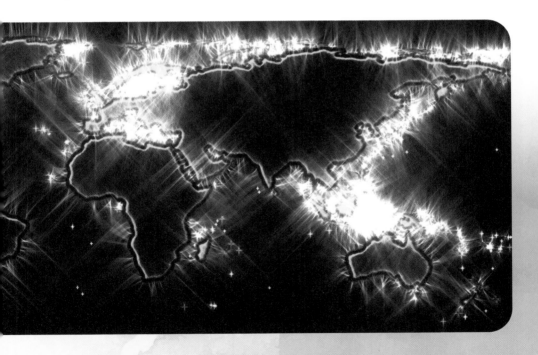

Meditation to attract the right job/career

The hardest part of any job or career is making a decision about what it is that you want to do. Once you have that part figured out, you can formulate what you need to do to achieve that outcome, and your energy also aligns to attract it to you. However, if you don't know what it is that you want to do with your life, or you feel as though you've spent some time in the wrong career and aren't sure what it is you want to do—only what you *don't* want to do—then this meditation should help you get some clarity.

1   Ensure that you are in a calm mood. Sip water. Breathe in and out in a gentle, conscious, yet unforced way.

2   Once you have reached a feeling of calm, close your eyes and state your desire to attract a career that's right for you.

3   Keeping your eyes closed, place your hands, one over the other, at your belly button with the palm of the hand closest to your body resting gently on your stomach.

4   As you breathe in and out, imagine that there is a force field of light that is emanating from your body on the in breath and contracting toward your body on the out breath. Then rest your hands, palms up, on your lap.

5   Imagine a column of sparkling yellow light coming down from the heavens and entering you at the top of your head.

6   Feel that light filling your body and emerging out of every pore. Let that light pool at your stomach and form a ball of light in your hands. Then, in your mind's eye, look into that ball of light as if you were looking into a crystal ball. See what comes up. Are you sitting at a desk, or are you outside? What are you wearing? Who are you working with? Try and see as much detail as possible.

7   Once you have seen some clear signs that may serve as leads for investigating a particular job or career, thank the Universe for the information, and push the ball of light above your head into the divine realm.

8   Then place your palms downward on your lap and rub them against your thighs. Gently open your eyes when you are ready.

TIPS

Once you've been given some leads from this meditation about what you should be doing, remember to do some conscious research into what you've been shown.

◎ It may be that you saw an animal in your meditation. If so, this won't necessarily mean that you should become a vet or a zookeeper. It may be that you have to embody the qualities of the animal that you saw.

◎ Fill out some job applications and investigate employment agencies. While you might not know exactly what you want to do, your meditation will start to attract opportunities.

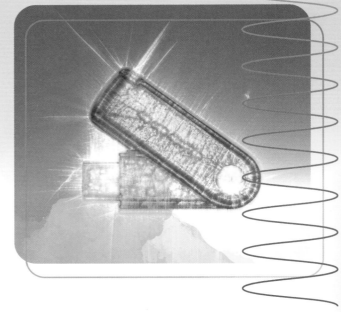

◎ Stay positive—don't give up!

Meditation to attract new opportunities

You may be trying to sell a property, or you may want to move to another country. However, you feel stagnated and can't see how to move forward with your plans. This meditation, when done every day for a month, will bring forward new opportunities that can help you achieve your goal. You may find that what you thought you wanted wasn't right for you after all, and this new opportunity will present fresh ideas on a way forward.

1   Ensure that you are in a calm mood. Sip water. Breathe in and out in a gentle, conscious, yet unforced way.

2   Once you have reached a feeling of calm, close your eyes and state your intention to be able to attract the opportunities that are right for you. You can be specific if you require an opportunity in a particular area, for example, a buyer for your house or a home to rent abroad.

3   Keeping your eyes closed, place your hands, one over the other, at your belly button with the palm of the hand closest to your body resting gently on your stomach.

4 As you breathe in and out, imagine that there is a force field of light that is emanating from your body on the in breath and contracting toward your body on the out breath. Then rest your hands, palms up, on your lap.

5 Now visualize the force field of light around you growing brighter and larger. Imagine that it is pulsing with a pure attractive energy. This is now magnetized and aligned to all those opportunities that are the very best for you.

6 Say out loud: "I trust the Universe to bring me what I need, in a loving manner. Thank you."

7 Turn your palms downward on your lap and rub them against your thighs. Gently open your eyes when you are ready.

8 Keep an eye out for anything that looks like it might be the opportunity you requested. It is not enough to simply do a meditation; you must also take actions in the mundane everyday world.

Further Reading

Advanced Studies of the Human Aura: How to Charge Your Energy Field with Light and Spiritual Radiance by David Christopher Lewis (Meru Pr, 2013)

Auras and How to Read Them by Sarah Bartlett (Collins and Brown, 2000)

Black Holes and Energy Pirates by Jesse Reeder (Gateway, 2001)

Chakras by Julian Flanders (Arcturus, 2020)

Energy Secrets by Alla Svirinskaya (Hay House, 2005)

How to Read the Aura by W.E. Butler (Thorsons, 1979)

Intermediate Studies of the Human Aura by Djwal Kul (Summit University Press, 1976)

Man Visible and Invisible by C.W. Leadbeater (1903)

Own Your Energy by Alla Svirinskaya (Hay House, 2019)

Studies of the Human Aura by Kuthumi (Summit University Press, 1976)

The Etheric Body of Man by Laurence J. Bendit & Phoebe D. Bendit (Quest, 1990)

The Etheric Double by Arthur E. Powell (Theosophical Publishing House, 1925)

The Inner Life by C.W. Leadbeater (1910)

The Science of the Aura by S.G.J. Ouseley (L.N. Fowler & Co, 1949)

Understanding Auras by Joseph Ostrom (HarperCollins, 1987)

Working with Auras by Jane Struthers (Godsfield Press, 2006)

Your Electro-Vibratory Body by Victor R. Beasley (University of the Trees Press, 1975)

ONLINE RESOURCES

College of Psychic Studies: collegeofpsychicstudies.co.uk

The Theosophical Society: theosophicalsociety.org.uk

Aloha International: huna.org

Index

Crystals

Crystals

How to use their
healing powers

———— ❉ ————

Emily Anderson

SIRIUS

To my boys Jake and Ethan

Images courtesy of Shutterstock and Pixabay.

SIRIUS

This edition published in 2021 by Sirius Publishing, a division of
Arcturus Publishing Limited,
26/27 Bickels Yard, 151–153 Bermondsey Street,
London SE1 3HA

ISBN: 978-1-3988-1321-2
AD007327US

Printed in China

Contents

Introduction

Crystal healers believe the earth contains within it the wisdom to heal our modern ills. Stare a while at a sparkly geode of amethyst or handle a smooth, perfect pebble of jade and they claim you will not just see the beauty in the stone, but also sense the energy it is emitting.

It is thought that a well-placed crystal can help us boost the energy of a place, calm our children, and enable us to have a good night's sleep. Used for centuries all over the world for healing, psychic divination, decoration, and spiritual development, crystals have a timeless power and attraction.

Today we use them in water bottles, in healing treatments, and to counteract the effects of electromagnetic fields in modern life. These crystalline allies continue to capture our imaginations and give us tangible ways of connecting to the spiritual realms.

This book will show you how crystals can help ground you, energize you or open up your intuition. Placed in the right area of your home, they are believed to attract abundance, love or psychic powers. Through right intention, focus, positioning and belief, you can use crystals to create genuine magic in your life.

However, it should be said here that the ideas and suggestions in this book are within the spiritual realm and are not intended to be a substitute for conventional medical help. Always consult your doctor before undertaking any alternative therapy to ensure that there are no counter-indications for your health.

History of crystal use

Crystals have always been sought after by nobility, used in spell-work by witches and mystics, and held in high regard both aesthetically and energetically. Until medieval times, garments—especially those of soldiers and explorers—had empowering amulets woven into them while incantations were chanted, to keep the wearer safe from harm and help wounds heal quicker. During the Middle Ages, healing gems were placed on saints' shrines and given religious as well as magical powers. In St Paul's Cathedral, in London, the sapphire on St Erkinwald's shrine was said to cure any visitors' eye diseases.

Native Americans believed positive energies from gemstones could be passed from one species to another, crystal to human to animal, in what they called a sacred hoop or circle of existence. Such traditional societies believed crystals to be conscious. Their interactive, supportive energies were said to amplify and focus our innate healing and intuitive abilities.

Lapis lazuli used in an Eye of Horus design for a woman's necklace in Ancient Egypt.

The book of Genesis in the Old Testament has one of the earliest references to a healing stone, which belonged to Abraham. This stone was reported to immediately cure any sick person who looked at it. In the Papyrus Ebers, from about 2500BCE, the healing properties of certain gems are listed. Rubies are thought to help liver and spleen diseases, lapis lazuli was made into eye balm, while emeralds were used for curing dysentery.

Even Plato, the Greek philosopher who lived from 427 to 347BCE, talked of crystals as being made by the stars, and planets converting decayed material into the most perfect gemstones, which were then ruled by these planets. If the Sun was in a certain constellation or the moon or another planet ascending at the time of engraving a crystal, it would make it even more powerful. It's believed that stones, including moonstone and topaz, strengthen in power during a waxing moon (the time between a new and full moon, when the moon appears to be getting bigger), peaking in healing ability when the moon is full.

Ancient Egyptians, the Chinese and alchemists up until the 18th century added crushed crystals to medicines, believing strongly in the physical and medical healing properties of gems. Over 200 gems and crystals that could be used in healing were listed in the Greek pharmacist Dioscorides' *De Materia Medica*. And the first Roman chronicler, Pliny, includes older crystal teachings in his *Natural History* and elaborates on the theory that the size and substance of the special stones used were important in the healing of different diseases. Despite the demise of other forms of traditional medicine practices, crystal healing remained popular far longer.

Does size matter?

Many crystals have electromagnetic energy fields, making them like a magnet. It may be that the larger crystal transmits more energy, but a smaller crystal can emit energy just as effectively with the right conscious intent and focused direction, when you become expert at doing so. Working with smaller gemstones is simply more practical, especially when you want to lay them on the body, or wear or carry them as a magic talisman.

In a spacious home, you can have a large piece sitting in the corner of a room or you can dedicate a small windowsill as seen here—both are beautiful and powerful.

Most experts and practitioners agree that a crystal of any size, rough or smooth, has healing properties. Clearly, the ancients would only have used the rough gems found in caves, deep in the earth, whereas today you can easily buy sparkly, domed geodes or smaller gems tumbled

and polished into perfectly smooth shapes. You can get rose quartz in the shape of hearts, or clear quartz made into a pyramid. While a crystal wand, made into a point, directs energy better, a rough or smooth texture doesn't matter when it comes to the power of crystals.

Whatever the shape or size, the healing and transformative properties of the stone come from the crystal itself and not its size; it's about how you work with them. Using them with love and clear, positive intention magnifies the benefits of any stone. You just need to make sure they are as close to genuine natural crystals as possible, for there are many imitations around nowadays.

Crystals found in nature have flaws and unequal coloring. They change over time, fading, becoming cloudy or veined over years of use. These gems develop naturally deep in the Earth, in rivers or cliffs, over a long period of time without any intervention. Specific types of crystals are found in particular locations; for example, turquoise is found in desert areas and created when water interacts with rock containing copper, aluminum and phosphorus. It is quite rare, so usually very expensive. Don't be fooled into thinking less expensive howlite that has been dyed to look like turquoise is the real thing. Dyed gems can look obviously dyed, in too-bright colors, or more natural. Many stones, including agate, howlite, jasper, quartz, dalmatian stone, and granite are very often dyed to boost their visual appeal, without really taking away anything from their quality. Even in Pliny's *Natural History*, it is recorded that gems were boiled in honey to enhance their appearance. Most rubies and sapphires have been treated in some way to improve their color, and emeralds often have their fractures filled and clarity improved.

Synthetic gems can be found more and more. They're not strictly fakes, as they contain the same chemical properties of raw gems but are created in laboratories in a condensed amount of time, and often seem more vibrant or uniform in color. They're also cheaper, but won't hold quite the same quality of energy as natural stones formed over centuries by the earth.

Fake crystals are not made of the same materials at all. They can look too perfect and can be cast from plastic, resin, ceramic or even painted rocks, just designed to look the same as real crystals. If there are bubbles in the gem, it's likely to be glass. Other methods of imitating crystals are with composites, which take the real mineral and just use it to coat glass or another rock.

The best way to avoid anything but the genuine item is to buy from reputable crystal shops or trusted experts. Ask where the crystal you like is from and have a really good, close look at it. Check its appearance and, most importantly, how it feels to you.

Choosing your crystals or rather letting them choose you

Do some research online or in books, or just browse around some crystal shops, and you will find certain crystals attract you much more than others. These are the ones for you. If you find yourself picking one up and you can't put it down, purchase it if you can, as it fits perfectly with your needs and desires at this time.

Cleansing and charging your gems

Crystals naturally pick up energy from their surroundings and anyone who's handled them. So, before you use them, you need to cleanse them – and then again at least every month, more if you're using them for intense healing sessions – to keep them working at optimum power.

There are many different ways to cleanse a crystal, and some are very specific to each stone. Check first that your crystal won't be damaged by the method you choose; some are delicate and can disintegrate in salt water, for example, or fade in too much sunlight. Here are the main ways to cleanse crystals:

✧ If your crystal is hard, and not likely to be harmed by water, a quick way to cleanse it is to hold it under running water for a few minutes or immerse it in the sea or a river.

✧ Most crystals like to be charged by the full moon's light or sunlight. Leave your gems outside on the night of a full moon and the following day so they soak up a full night and day of bright moon and sunlight.

✧ Put your crystals in a pot of herbs generally used for healing

and purifying, such as rosemary, sage or lavender. A day immersed in any of these scented leaves or flowers will absorb any dense and unwanted energy.

✧ If you live near stone circles, ancient burial mounds or other sacred sites, take your crystal there straight after the sun rises and lay them out on a flat stone if possible. Leave them for at least half an hour, and the negative energies in the gems will soak into the stones, while the power from the area will empower them.

✧ Smudging—wafting the smoke from a special, cleansing bundle of sagebrush or cedar—is an ancient way of cleansing your energy and environment, and it works very well for crystals too. When you have your smudge stick gently smoking, simply pass each crystal through the purifying smoke a few times so the cleansing scent is absorbed.

✧ You can also buy special crystal cleansing sprays from shops specializing in alternative spirituality, and one drop or spray on each stone should do the trick.

Now that your crystals are cleansed, they are ready to be charged with your intention, whether that's to heal others, connect with your higher consciousness or manifest certain things in your life. To do this, simply ask your crystal to do what is needed for your personal or spiritual growth, and to always work for the highest good for all. Whatever your request from your gems might be, it's worth adding "this or something better" so that the outcome is left up to higher powers, and may even surprise you with its brilliance.

After working with a crystal for a specific purpose, thank it for its help if you've finished the work, or ask that it keep acting on your behalf, either when you use it again for the same purpose, or just while you go about your day.

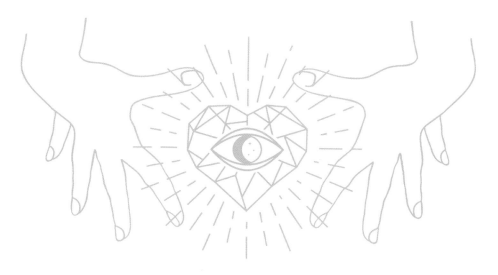

The Best Crystals For Meditation

Meditating using crystals will deepen your meditation practice, increase your intuition, and help you to connect with higher consciousness, spirit guides, and even angels.

Meditating with crystals

Creating a daily meditation practice is incredibly beneficial. It brings peace, patience, clarity and relaxation. Add some crystals to that practice and you can develop your spirituality further—heightening your intuition, encouraging telepathy or communing with the angelic realm, spirit guides or your ancestors.

The following section lists ten of the best crystals to meditate with to expand your consciousness further than you dreamed possible. Find out which crystals resonate with you the most, or choose according to which psychic skills or mystical experience you'd most like to have. Maybe you'd like to try placing a crystal on each chakra for a full-body boost. See the section on page 34 to find out more.

GETTING STARTED

✦ Find somewhere quiet where you can be undisturbed and comfortable for ten to 20 minutes or more. Lie down on the floor, or sit upright on a pillow or a chair.

✦ Hold your chosen crystals in your hands. Feel their energy permeate your body and the space around you.

✦ Set an intention for the crystals in this meditation. Visualize those intentions in detail in your mind, and imagine this charging up your crystals with purpose to help you in whatever path you've chosen at this time. Continue holding the crystals in your hands, or you can place them on the chakras they clear and strengthen. Or simply place them by your side to work their magic beside you.

✧ Now, close your eyes and relax. As with all meditation, begin by focusing on your breathing. Allow yourself to take some nice deep breaths in, and some slow breaths out. Inhale. Exhale.

✧ Allow the energy of the crystal to have an effect— but don't force it or worry if it doesn't. Just continue relaxing and breathing deeply, and see what unfolds. You may get a strong sense to do something new in your life; you might hear messages from other beings; you could even have visions of past-life experiences. Just witness it all, knowing you are safe.

POWERFUL EFFECTS

✧ When you feel like you've come to the end of your meditation, count down from 10 to one to bring your awareness back into the room. Wriggle your fingers and toes, or stretch, keeping your eyes closed. Now, imagine your feet are like the roots of a tree going deep into the ground. Your body is strong and rooted to the earth. Hold this visualization for a few minutes to strongly ground your energy back into the present moment, necessary after traveling to other realms or being in a relaxed state of bliss for a while.

✧ When you're ready, move slowly from your position and go about your day. Have a notebook nearby to note down any experiences you had that resonate, or any questions that have arisen. You may find yourself having sudden realizations or epiphanies about issues in your life.

Keep meditating with your favorite crystals and you will gain a stronger sense of purpose in your life. You may connect with a particular spirit guide or angel who will help you on your path. Your dreams will probably become more vivid, with clear messages or symbolism that you remember easily on waking. Your ability to sense what's about to happen or what someone is going to say or do may be stronger. Your connection with others, your creativity and your destiny will become better than it has ever been. All because you took the time to simply be with some of the most powerful, life-changing tools on our planet.

Amethyst

BEST FOR:
Developing your spirituality, deepening meditation, and enhancing creativity.

LOOKS:
Pale lavender to deep purple quartz, sometimes opaque, sometimes transparent, with white or clear streaks.

Amethyst is one of the most spiritual stones, and has a very high vibration. Used by ancient royalty to encourage sobriety and spiritual grounding, this purple quartz will help you tap into a deeper, more centered, spirituality. It helps still the mind of mental chatter, calm anxieties, and inspire a deeper meditative state. This will enable you to really tune into your intuition, and it will also allow your psychic side to develop.

Add an amethyst geode to your meditation altar, where you can sit next to it and feel its powerful calming effects, removing any tension or stress in your life. Alternatively, lie down to meditate with a smaller stone placed on your third eye, as amethyst opens this and the crown chakras, further enhancing your psychic abilities.

To increase your awareness further in meditation, sit holding a single stone or small clusters in your left hand, with the point toward your left arm, to draw the calming spiritual energy into your body.

The ancient Egyptians made amulets from amethyst as a form of prayer and to protect against harm. It is still used today as a protection stone, to ward off psychic attack by creating a protective shield of light around the body.

Hold a sizable chunk in your left hand, resting on your right hand, while sitting comfortably and allowing your breath to deepen and your worries to melt away. Imagine the purple amethyst energy forming a protective light around your body as you travel safely into other worlds in your mind. Meditating in this way with an amethyst can also bring success and help you focus on new endeavors. Its ability to expand your higher mind means it can boost your creativity, imagination and passion for new projects.

A soothing stone, especially for children, it can help relieve insomnia and curb nightmares. Place it under your child's pillow to help them drift into a peaceful sleep. Or rub a point of amethyst counterclockwise in the center of the forehead to alleviate fear of the dark and recurring dreams.

Worth wearing as a pendant due to its powers of protection from negativity, it can also help soothe your spirit after the death of a loved one and bring your emotions back to balance after any disturbance.

Angelite

BEST FOR:
Communing with the angels, developing telepathy and clairvoyance, and for clear communication.

LOOKS:
White exterior with light blue inside.

Angelite is highly evolved celestite that has been compressed for millions of years to form nodules. It is made of calcium sulphate and found in Peru. This stone of awareness and tranquility helps soothe excessive emotions and create a deeper inner serenity. Vibrating at the frequency of benevolence, its energy can greatly assist during difficult times and guide you on your spiritual journey.

Sit next to, or hold, a piece of angelite crystal when you meditate to receive the love and guidance imbued in this rare gem. Feel the love and support that the angels can give you.

If you have a meditation altar, place a piece of angelite on it and let your gaze rest upon it, eyes half open. Tune into your angelic guides or guardians from the higher planes, bringing you their wisdom and guidance, in messages, symbols or general sensations. Meditate regularly using angelite to increase any psychic abilities, including channeling, clairvoyance, mediumship and spiritual healing.

Angelite is a helpful stone for astrologers and anyone involved in giving readings or spiritual counseling, as it encourages clear and balanced communication of insights. Have it beside you if you do any readings for others, to help you share messages from spirit guides, the stars or cards, with compassion and kindness.

Connected to the crown, third eye and throat chakras, it aligns them all, bringing you closer to the angelic realms. Wear it on a choker-style necklace to clear negativity from the throat chakra in particular, to help soften your speech and avoid rambling. Wearing it here can also help bring peace in relationship conflicts. Physically, it can help you with emotional overeating and healing broken bones when worn on the body or through crystal healing.

This gentle gem increases the spiritual nature of your dreams and helps you interpret their guidance correctly. It also assists with tuning into the Akashic records (where everything that has ever happened is recorded in the etheric realm) in your dreams. Place a piece of angelite next to your bed to help you stay lucid in dreams and remember the wisdom revealed in them when you wake up. Make sure you keep your angelite crystal dry. It's so delicate, it can be damaged by water.

Azurite

BEST FOR:
Connecting with the heavenly realm, reaching the quiet stillness at the heart of meditation, receiving healing and psychic experiences.

LOOKS:
Bright to deep blue and indigo, sometimes with light blue streaks.

Known as the "stone of heaven" by the ancient Chinese, azurite connects our worldly realm to that of the gods, and to the void beyond all awareness that all meditators seek for true healing and psychic gifts. By opening up the third eye chakra, azurite expands all intuitive abilities and brings ancient and advanced knowledge forth in meditation.

It can enhance your dreams, take you into a channeling state and help you astral-travel safely. Elevating the powers of the mind, it can clear tension, confusion, and bring forth new perspectives, allowing you to envisage and manifest exciting possibilities in your life.

Azurite has been used to guide people to enlightenment ever since the earliest civilizations began. The Mayans used it to spark their mystical side, while Native Americans would meditate with it to contact their spirit guides and receive messages. In Atlantis and Ancient Egypt, it was only priests and priestesses who knew the full power of such a special psychic stone.

The potent energies in this gem are better released through touching, so hold a smoothed stone of azurite in your hands during meditation and ask for its help. It makes a great touchstone during a past-life regression session to journey successfully back to previous lives. Whether you wear it or carry it in your pocket, be sure to smooth your fingers over it often.

This stunning stone will inspire new interests and connections with others. It also encourages an aspiration for more knowledge and awareness. Place one on your desk to touch often and feel the invigorating, mind-expanding energies. Great to use when studying for a test, or thinking up new ideas for a project, it's believed to boost concentration and memory retention. It's definitely a stone to discreetly rub between your fingers during an interview or presentation to focus the mind. Azurite is a good crystal for the elderly to wear, or meditate with, to fortify their mental alertness and overall brain health.

This bright blue stone clears the throat chakra so the new ideas and experiences you've just received can be perfectly communicated. Wear it as a necklace or place it on the throat area when lying down in meditation. Its clairvoyant energy makes azurite perfect for a pendulum, for dowsing accurate and objective answers to questions.

Black Tourmaline

BEST FOR:
Protecting against negative thoughts, energies and radiation from electronics, also for grounding, easing panic attacks and motion sickness.

LOOKS:
Black or very deep blue-black, found in column structures.

Black tourmaline, also known as Schorl, is one of the most common crystals used in meditation due to its ability to keep you grounded. It connects the root chakra to the Earth's electromagnetic field, essential in these times of shifting energies on the planet.

This shamanic stone, used by ancient magicians when doing spell-work, provides a protective shield against any negative entities or bad vibes from people or places.

Known also as the "etheric bodyguard," it protects and purifies the etheric body, keeping you safe while you explore the spiritual realm. Place a smooth stone of black tourmaline in each hand or one in your left hand and a piece of selenite crystal in your right hand, to cleanse

your aura while you meditate.

Wear a black tourmaline brooch on your left side—where this crystal enters the aura—if you find yourself in unpleasant surroundings or mixing with angry, complaining or draining people.

Sit in meditation surrounded by a grid of black tourmaline stones to clear the mind of unwanted self-talk, cleanse the emotions and body of impurities, and rid the spirit of anything weighing you down. An essential crystal for anyone suffering from anxiety, depression or anger issues, try sleeping with some in your pillowcase to help clear you overnight.

If there's an area of your home where you feel more negativity, place a large piece of black tourmaline on its own there and let it transmute the energy around it. Working with black tourmaline promotes a sense of self-confidence and personal power.

Black tourmaline is believed to protect the body from harmful radiation and electromagnetic waves from gadgets such as computers and cell phones. Place a large piece of it next to any electrical device, or wear black tourmaline on your body when working on electrical devices for long periods of time.

Rub a piece of black tourmaline and it will become electrically charged, with one end positive and the other negative. It will then attract or repel dust particles, for example. It aligns the energy centers in your body to enable healing light to channel through you, increase physical vitality, and inspire a clear-headed and positive attitude.

Blue Calcite

BEST FOR:
Soothing wrought emotions, promoting inner peace.
Helps with recuperation and clear communication.

LOOKS:
Opaque light blue and white.

The simplest forms of calcite are pure white, but other minerals in the compound create various colors, with light blue calcite being particularly soothing on the eye, the body and the emotions. If you need restoration and want to bring your life into balance, use blue calcite in meditation.

Its calming energy is beneficial for those suffering from anxiety, stress, or after a major life event. It releases negative emotions and encourages relaxation and healing. Sleeping with a chunk of blue calcite on your bedside table can work as a natural sedative, helping you drift off into a restful sleep, even after trauma or during times of mental anguish.

Blue calcite is a powerful purifier, and can be used to help absorb old behaviors or thought patterns and send back increased motivation and positive energy, transforming your life for the better. Meditating with blue calcite creates a more optimistic outlook by helping you see the perfection inherent in all of life.

Sit calmly, holding a blue calcite crystal in your hands, and say: *"I am connecting to a calming universal energy"* as many times as feels comforting, until you feel fully relaxed. In this state, your natural, creative side will manifest with new ideas and interests.

Place this soft blue gem on the third eye chakra while lying down meditating to activate strong intuition and inner vision. Blue calcite enhances the vividness of your dreams and helps you understand their symbolism. Because blue calcite also opens and strengthens the throat chakra, it will help you clearly communicate any insights you receive. Balancing this chakra can smooth relationship disagreements, enabling you to find new ways of looking at situations and resolve issues with others in a calm and patient way.

Being a powerful energy amplifier, blue calcite is also a good stone for distance healing. Send healing thoughts during meditation while holding a blue calcite crystal, and they are sure to reach the recipient.

Also known as the "stone of the mind," blue calcite increases memory and learning capabilities. Choose this stone to meditate with daily if you are studying, or in any academic field, as it will help you retain information more easily.

Blue Topaz

BEST FOR:
Peacefulness, truth, connecting with spiritual beings.

LOOKS:
Light blue transparent.

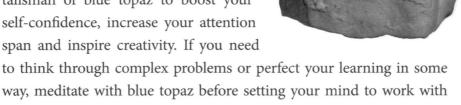

With its gentle frequency, blue topaz brings peace, helping to calm your emotions. Yet it also subtly energizes the mind, brings clarity and helps avoid procrastination. Wear a talisman of blue topaz to boost your self-confidence, increase your attention span and inspire creativity. If you need to think through complex problems or perfect your learning in some way, meditate with blue topaz before setting your mind to work with renewed dynamism.

Use blue topaz to connect with the spiritual realm and hear Divine wisdom clearly. Meditating with it will also enhance any affirmations and visualizations, and discern what is genuinely true for you. Sitting with blue topaz for some time will deepen your meditation practice and allow the physical body to assimilate wisdom from the higher mind. It will strengthen your inner guidance and improve your psychic abilities, making it a great gem to have by your side if you give readings to others.

When lying down to meditate, place a blue topaz stone on the throat or third eye chakra to help you make clear distinctions between what you would like or not like in your life. This will also enable you to consciously articulate any feelings and thoughts you want to express with regards to your personal desires.

Traditionally a gem of love and abundance, blue topaz can support you emotionally so you feel ready to receive affection from wherever it manifests. It's a soothing crystal to help you relax on all levels, enhancing and quickening spiritual development where it may have been blocked, and helping manifest your dreams.

The gentle blue color of this crystal can help you see your truth, and will highlight any behavior pattern or blueprint you've been following that has kept you from fully being your true self. It will cleanse the aura, encourage forgiveness, and disconnect you from any doubts you have about which path to take. Wearing this gem will connect you more to your higher consciousness, so it can lead you to your genuine aspirations.

Blue topaz can help you see the bigger picture of a situation as well as the details. Set goals while sitting quietly with blue topaz by imagining how they will play out on both a small and large scale in your life. Then fill your crystal with that creative, can-do energy and trust that the good things will unfold naturally while you allow yourself to just "be."

WHICH CRYSTALS FOR WHICH CHAKRAS?

Choose the right crystal for each of your chakras—the energy centers that run up and down your body—and you can balance and strengthen your whole system. Each chakra has specific stones that work best with it, so choose the one that resonates with you the most. Place each one onto the specific chakra while lying down, let your breathing and body relax, and the crystals will do the rest.

CROWN
Top of head: spirituality,
reaching higher dimensions, pure bliss
AMETHYST, CLEAR QUARTZ, SELENITE

THIRD EYE
Between the eyebrows: strengthens intuition, imagination,
decision-making and sense of purpose
AMETHYST, BLACK OBSIDIAN, BLUE CALCITE

THROAT
Center of neck: clear communication,
expressing your truth and feelings
BLUE CALCITE, BLUE TOPAZ, LAPIS LAZULI,
AQUAMARINE, TURQUOISE

HEART
Center of chest: self-acceptance,
love, joy, inner peace, trust
ROSE QUARTZ, JADE, MOLDAVITE

SOLAR PLEXUS
Two inches above belly button: enhances creativity,
confidence, personal power
MALACHITE, CALCITE, TOPAZ, CITRINE

SACRAL
Two inches below belly button:
sense of pleasure, sexuality and abundance
CITRINE, CARNELIAN, MOONSTONE

ROOT
Base of spine: helps you feel grounded,
balanced and independent
TIGER'S EYE, BLACK TOURMALINE, HEMATITE

Clear Quartz

BEST FOR:
Amplifying energy, raising your vibration, enhancing intuition and psychic ability.

LOOKS:
Clear crystal, shimmery in the light.

The most common yet most powerful mineral on earth, clear quartz is known as the "master healer," and was key to the development of many ancient civilizations. A staple spiritual and magical tool for Celts, Mayans, Aztecs, Egyptians and Native Americans, many believed these stones to be alive, incarnations of the Divine. They were believed to have a great power for healing and for raising consciousness.

Clear quartz magnifies the power of any other crystal as well as the body's natural energy, making it an essential stone for meditation and healing. While it stimulates the whole chakra system, it is especially good for opening the crown chakra. Regularly meditating with clear quartz will help expand your consciousness, connect with the angelic realm or remember past lives. Sleep next to some clear quartz and let its mesmerizing quality help you drift into a deep sleep, full of memorable and meaningful dreams.

Sitting quietly, place a quartz crystal on the heart chakra will transform any emotional blocks into self-acceptance and love. Placed on the third eye during meditation, clear quartz will increase mental clarity, filter out distractions and enable you to focus on the pure bliss of stillness beyond. Here, your intuition and psychic abilities can manifest.

Program clear quartz with your intention for your meditation, such as to connect with your spirit guides, and it will assist with this every time you use it.

Achieve any goal by sending the feeling of the desired result into the quartz during meditation. It will remember and magnify that energy, bringing forth opportunities for that outcome to manifest the more you meditate with it.

Clear quartz is used a lot in technology including watches, radio transmitters and receivers and memory chips in computers because it can store, amplify and transform energy. Place this healing gem on your desk if you work with computers or other electronic devices, as it repels the harmful effects of radiation from such equipment. Clear quartz also cleanses and protects the aura by removing positive ions and producing negative ions instead.

Because it's such an enhancer of energies, make sure you cleanse your clear quartz regularly in one of a variety of ways. You can soak it in a saltwater solution overnight, leave it in the sunshine, or smudge it with sage smoke.

Labradorite

BEST FOR:
Magic, protection, courage, traveling between realms.

LOOKS:
Gray, murky green, black, or grayish white with a rainbow of colored layers from bright blue and pale green, flashes of gold and coppery red.

Discovered in Labrador, Canada in 1770, labradorite's mystical and magical powers are mind-blowing. Looking like the Aurora Borealis—where the Inuit people believe the crystal came from—its "labradorescence" of colors flashes out of its mostly gray exterior. Underneath what appears to be a fairly ordinary stone is an array of reflective, spectral colors, symbolic of labradorite's ability to allow spiritual seekers and shamen to move through the dark, unseen realms while still keeping their own light strong.

Known as a "stone of magic," it's the go-to crystal for healers, magicians, and anyone who wants transformation, self-discovery and spiritual adventure. It helps with spirit communication, accessing Akashic records and understanding past lives.

Labradorite acts as a protective talisman for those who travel between worlds seeking knowledge and guidance, ensuring their soul

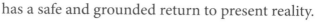

has a safe and grounded return to present reality.

Wearing or carrying labradorite allows your natural magical powers to surface, as well as bringing forgotten memories to light to help you move on from them. Meditating with it will awaken innate psychic abilities, such as telepathy, clairvoyance and awareness of synchronicity.

Amplify this stone's protection energy when journeying in meditation by imagining it transforming your body into a magical rainbow body shining with hues of blue, green, purple, violet and gold. Ask labradorite to activate this array of color within you, keep your vibration high and open all chakras.

You must use this crystal with intentions of developing a higher awareness, as labradorite wants you to expand your knowledge of both the light and the dark. Also known as the "stone of balance," it will help you face your darker, subconscious self and balance the two extremes within you, enabling you to shine even brighter after traveling inward.

Labradorite is most potent during dusk and dawn, when nature displays a similar spectrum of color and you can feel its energy more. Sit outside in the changing light, and see all humanity as one "being of light" transcending limitations of the past, and fears for the future, to see the infinite possibilities in the now. Part of this pure light, you can allow yourself to just "be."

Moldavite

BEST FOR:
Powerful transformation, healing, protection.

LOOKS:
Deep, forest green, olive, greenish brown and glassy, with carved, etched or wrinkled patterns in raw unpolished stones.

Found only in the Czech Republic, moldavite has extraterrestrial connections. It was created when a meteor crashed into the earth nearly 15 million years ago in the Bohemian Plateau, where pieces are scattered throughout the area. The shapes of moldavite found back up its molten origins: most are round to very flat, drop-like or disc shapes, spheres, ovals or spirals—all common liquid splash patterns.

Once as prized as emerald, its usage goes back to the Neolithic people of Eastern Europe, in 25,000BCE. They used it not only for arrowheads and cutting tools, but also as an amulet for protection, good fortune and fertility. It was found in the archaeological site of the Venus of Willendorf, the oldest known Goddess statue. A powerful addition to any meditation session, moldavite is an energy amplifier that opens up all the chakras, enhancing spiritual growth. Called a "stone of connectivity," connecting universal and earthly energies, it increases connection to intuition, telepathy and guidance from spiritual realms.

Meditating with this gem regularly will ease doubts and worries, especially about money, giving you insights into new solutions to any problems and helping you tap into the magic of the universe.

Moldavite has an intense vibration, often felt quickly and dramatically, that can take some getting used to. The first time you hold moldavite, it can feel warm to the touch, a feeling first felt in the hand and then through the body. It activates the heart chakra, felt as a pounding pulse, sweating or flushing of the face, and encourages cathartic release of outdated beliefs and ideas that no longer serve you. Let the tears or laughter flow, and know this crystal will help the heart and mind work together to change your life for the better.

Carrying a piece of moldavite or wearing it as jewelry will rejuvenate you and slow down aging. Vibrating at this heightened frequency means more beneficial synchronicities will come your way to help you transform and heal. But get used to wearing it slowly and take your time, as it can lead to light-headedness.

If you sometimes find it hard living on this planet, with its heavy energy, suffering and wild emotions, lie down with a piece of moldavite on your heart area. It will help you know the reasons why you are incarnated here at this time and give you a renewed sense of purpose and fulfillment.

Selenite

BEST FOR:

Deep connection to higher realms, improving telepathy and psychic insight.

LOOKS:

Pure white or translucent, grows naturally in wands, sometimes in pairs.

Selenite is named after the Greek Moon Goddess Selene and, much like the moon, represents tranquility, blessings and heavenly light. A stone for females—mothers in particular—it boosts libido, fertility and fidelity. It encourages commitment, communication between couples and helps you see through deception.

Naturally found growing in long, slender wands, selenite has a high vibration that activates the crown chakra, helping you connect with ancestors, angels and ascended masters. Meditating often with selenite will bring a deep peace, boost your telepathic and psychic skills, and protect your aura.

A selenite wand is a great tool for directing your intention and energy outward to others or the wider world, in prayer or manifestation exercises. Selenite wands are also used to sense energy blocks in the chakras and then send the crystal's pure light to clear the channel.

You can also create energy grids at home or outside with these wands. Lying in the center of a selenite grid means nothing negative will come to you, and you can experience true spiritual ascension.

When activating your selenite, try gently stroking it. To receive psychic insight, lie in meditation with a wand on the heart chakra pointing at your head and another on the floor with the point just touching your crown chakra. Breathe deeply and feel the calm clarity this crystal brings. In your mind, you may meet spiritual beings with messages for you, or receive visual symbols or stories about past lives or the future.

Alternatively, sit upright, breathing in deeply and imagining white light filling your body, allowing yourself to relax. Hold your selenite in your left hand and place your right hand underneath the left, cradling your crystal in your lap. Look gently at your selenite and attune yourself to its pure white light.

Next, slowly place your crystal on top of your head (the crown chakra) and let the white light of the selenite enter the crown. Move the gem to your third eye chakra and hold it there for a few minutes. Know that you are safe, and let your mind journey where it wants—to familiar places, through the stars, or channeling beings from other dimensions. Don't forget to ground yourself after communing with the cosmos. While selenite can be cleansed in water that the full moonlight has shone into, never leave it in water, as it will dissolve.

The Best Crystals For Manifestation

Whether you want a new job, more money or better relationships, use crystals to help you manifest the life you want.

Manifesting your desires

If you want to be more successful in your career, find a new partner or experience better health, then try manifesting with certain crystals.

Working with crystals will help you uncover and release any emotional blocks and challenges to the natural flow of abundance. Take time to meditate with the right one to focus inward, to discover what's stopping you from realizing your purpose and reaching your full potential. Perhaps it's fear, pain, sadness or exhaustion built up by past events and experiences, weighing heavy on your spirit. Take time to be kind to yourself and know that these feelings shall pass in time.

Remember to be grateful for all you already have. There is always something you can focus on in your present to be thankful for—a healthy body, a warm, safe home. Feeling gratitude for our life increases the flow of positive energy, bringing more wonderful things our way.

Meditating with crystals will bring clarity on what you really want in life, what changes you need to make to increase your luck and prosperity. They will connect with, cleanse and open up certain chakras to boost your energy and help attract the perfect situations and opportunities to you. Hold your chosen crystal while you meditate, or place it over its corresponding chakra to really feel the benefits of its stirring and proactive boost.

Manifestation is all about right timing and trusting that everything will work out as it's meant to, if you are open to the magic of the universe. Try setting an intention with a positive affirmation—charging a crystal to work for you. Imagine your life working out the way you want it to, and send that visualization into the crystal. Keep that charged crystal near you when you're working, or place it in your wallet to attract wealth and balance your spending.

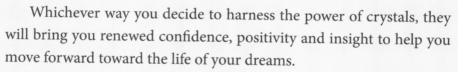

Try wearing your charged crystal as part of a necklace, set in a ring, brooch or earrings to stay in contact with its powerful manifesting energy all day long. This will empower you to make the right decisions to lead you on the right path, and to know that you do deserve the things you desire.

Whichever way you decide to harness the power of crystals, they will bring you renewed confidence, positivity and insight to help you move forward toward the life of your dreams.

Citrine

BEST FOR:
Enhancing career, creativity and communication, manifesting abundance.

LOOKS:
Pale yellow to amber and orange quartz.

Citrine is also called the sun stone, and holds the clear energy of the morning sunlight, bringing joy, abundance and optimism to all areas of life, especially career and finances.

Historically known as "the Merchant's Stone," and associated with the planet Mercury, citrine is believed to improve a person's sales talk, upping their wealth and success in business. Long ago, merchants placed this stone in their vaults to protect their money and attract more. Today, businesses can get a boost by placing a small piece of citrine by the cash register or computer, if that's where the money is made, to help boost income.

Citrine is also known to encourage wise spending decisions by strengthening intuition. It allows you to release past anger, fears of lack and destructive habits blocking abundance, and encourages you to see a brighter future ahead. This boosts self-esteem and helps you enjoy new things, leading you to create and act on new opportunities for more prosperity.

Try this ritual for extra prosperity:

At dawn, burn a yellow candle next to a piece of citrine. This will charge the stone with abundance energies. Once the candle is burned down, keep the fully charged crystal in your wallet to attract wealth.

A powerful stone for anyone involved in communications or expressive arts, citrine ignites creative imagination and willpower by opening up the sacral chakra. Activating your imagination is the first step toward manifestation, because you need to first envision the future you want to bring it into being.

Visualize and really feel your desire becoming reality while holding a piece of citrine in your dominant hand. Imagine this vision charging the stone with energy to help you put plans into action to make it all come into being.

From the sacral chakra, citrine's energy wakes up the solar plexus and the root chakra, helping all three to radiate the stone's sunlight. This ignites our will and energy to work hard and persevere to make things happen out of the ideas coming from the imagination.

Citrine transmutes rather than absorbs negativity, so it never needs to be cleansed. But to enhance its radiance, leave citrine in sunlight from dawn until midday, especially on the summer solstice. Just don't leave it in direct sunlight too often, as it can fade or crack.

Golden Topaz

BEST FOR:
Amplifying and manifesting spiritual intention, giving courage, wisdom and success.

LOOKS:
Golden yellow silicate, although topaz forms in yellow, gold, orange, red, blue, green, purple and brown.

Also known as imperial topaz, this golden gem is associated with opulence, luxury and generosity. Topaz means "fire" in Sanskrit, and this crystal harnesses the fire of the sun to radiate a gentle energy with a powerful pull. Traditionally worn as a charm to attract a wealthy lover, now it's more of a spiritually rich soul-mate magnet in love rituals, while also used as a talisman to attract money and prosperity. Hope to manifest true love and friendship, the right person at the right time to help boost career, plus courage, charisma and success when working with golden topaz. This crystal reaches greatest power as the moon waxes to full moon.

Topaz is a "crystal of potency," because it produces linked negative and positive currents that transmit attraction and manifestation to the ether. Request your desires to the universe and embed them into this crystal with your mind, and you'll receive clarity and focus on the path to take to reach those goals. Topaz is one of the best gems to empower you with positive affirmations and bring clear visualization of the future in meditation.

With its golden shimmer, Topaz lifts the spirits, helps you feel better about yourself and gives you the energy to turn ideas and intentions into action. It clears away fatigue and outdated emotions or habits weighing you down, and replaces this with peace and well-being. Topaz activates the root, sacral and solar plexus chakras, as well as the crown, which increases your likelihood of transforming your highest path into action and making it reality.

Sit quietly and tune into your topaz to connect consciously to the heavenly realm and receive divine guidance, letting that wisdom be stored in the gem for future manifestation. It will recharge you physically and spiritually, boosting your faith in what's to come, increasing your confidence and pride in your abilities while remaining open-hearted and generous. Anyone in public speaking, teaching, sales or philanthropy would benefit from carrying a piece of topaz with them or wearing it on a pendant, to ensure that they speak the truth with kindness and love.

Topaz is also known as the "gourmet's stone," because it increases sensitivity to taste and stimulates the taste buds. Sucking on a piece of topaz before a meal or wine can help you appreciate it even more.

Golden or Gold Sheen Obsidian

BEST FOR:

Boosting personal power, spiritual manifestation and earth healing.

LOOKS:

Dark brown or black obsidian filled with a golden metallic sheen or sparkly gold "cat's-eye" effect in bright light.

Obsidian, usually dark brown or black, is nature's glass, formed from volcanic lava hardened so fast no crystalline structure is formed. It's also called "volcano glass," "mirror of the Incas," and "Iceland agate." This golden kind of obsidian has a shimmery "chatoyancy," or cat's-eye effect, that can be seen in strong light and was created by the alignment of gas bubbles during its formation.

This gem connects to the root and especially solar plexus chakras, working here to highlight and clear any persistent, long-term negative feelings that have to do with conflicts of ego or abuse of power. If you ever feel cynical about life, this crystal will help you get over such despondency, caused by past unpleasant events or traumatic experiences. It's a grounded and protective gem to help you clear emotional blockages, and then get motivated to move forward again.

Before manifesting anything, sleep with golden obsidian under your pillow to help alleviate any anxiety or stress. Then meditate with it to get clear about what's holding you back from manifesting your desires. Allow the crystal's energy to purify your energy field of any negativity. See its golden light permeating your solar plexus and root chakras, and fill your whole body and aura with its illuminating power.

Once beliefs and habits that no longer serve you are cleared away, the opportunity for new experiences can come into your life. Wear golden obsidian to help focus on what you want and how to manifest it over time.

Golden obsidian is good to gaze into and see the future, as well as for getting to the heart of a problem in the present. As well as diagnosing psychological issues for healing, golden obsidian helps with earth healing, pinpointing the place of disruption in the earth's energy system. Reiki practitioners, shamen or those working in the healing arts choose golden obsidian to help highlight and focus on the spiritual and physical places that need healing.

This strong stone helps you tap into your personal power and aligns it with higher consciousness. Allow golden obsidian to influence you, and it may reveal hidden talents and your true purpose in life.

Green Aventurine

BEST FOR:
Creating opportunities, good luck and prosperity.

LOOKS:
Light to mid green, opaque, oxide quartz often containing bright inclusions of mica, giving it a metallic glisten, especially when polished.

Aventurine is usually green, but also forms in blue, red, reddish brown, orange, peach, yellow, silver gray or dusty purple. Its name comes from the Italian word for chance, and refers to an accidental sparkly inclusion into glass in the 1700s. This name was then later given to the natural stone with its bright shimmer caused by mica particles in the quartz.

Known as the "stone of opportunity," green aventurine is the crystal to have with you if you need some good luck—whether in a job interview, on a first date, or trying your luck in a casino.

It's believed to line up opportunities for the taking, helping you manifest wealth and prosperity. Meditate with green aventurine and you'll be given visions and insights into how you can be lucky and achieve your goals through hard work and determination. This in turn brings positivity and boosts self-esteem so you know you deserve the best people, things and opportunities in your life.

Green aventurine rebalances the heart chakra, helping you to better understand your needs and feel what your heart really wants to manifest. It clears away any heartache and emotional blockages caused by mistakes or setbacks, and releases harmful behavior patterns. It's a great comfort crystal in times of change, giving you faith that you'll get through anything, enabling you to see tough times as a chance for growth and to build resilience, trusting in the greater good.

Its soothing energy can calm anger and nervousness, get rid of everyday stresses and harmonize erratic emotions. By bringing you back into balance, you can better manifest what you want, from a place of well-being. By working often with green aventurine in your manifestation rituals, you become a leader in your life, with improved decision-making abilities, motivation and belief in your own talents.

With the help of aventurine giving you a renewed zest for life, you can create better luck and move forward with confidence that good things will happen. It will help you see that the positive energy you put out in the world comes back to you, which is what manifesting good outcomes is all about.

Cleanse green aventurine often, as it absorbs negative energy. Place it outside, buried in the earth a few inches deep, to fully recharge.

Green Jade

BEST FOR:
Healing the heart to attract love and friendship, balancing mind, body and spirit, calmly and confidently acting on your dreams.

LOOKS:
Dark green and glassy or lighter, dull and waxy depending on whether it's nephrite or jadeite.

Jade is the name given to two different minerals: glassy-looking nephrite, a calcium magnesium silicate, and jadeite, a sodium aluminum silicate with a waxier veneer. The best way to tell them apart is by tapping with a hard object: nephrite will chime a musical note, jadeite won't. But they both help protect your finances and attract more wealth.

Since ancient times, green jade has been used to bring wisdom, abundance and prosperity. It helps you gets rid of negativity and see yourself as you really are, full of loving potential. It soothes irritability, stops damaging self-talk and ends self-imposed limitations blocking abundance. This gem brings the mind, body and spirit into balance, enabling manifestation to happen more easily.

Green jade connects with your inner child, bringing purity, joy and spontaneity, from which all good ideas and creativity manifest. It gives you confidence, self-esteem and self-reliance.

At work, place some green jade on your desk to boost success, especially when trying to attract new business or negotiate a deal. If people are confusing you with facts or figures, jade will keep your mind sharp to discern the best outcome. It will stimulate new ideas and make tasks easier to undertake. Rub a small, smooth stone of green jade to bring calm if you're dealing with difficult situations or overwhelmed with daily events.

This revered crystal is a powerful heart healer, softening and balancing any upset. Hold it to your heart center and you will feel its strong energies pulsing out through your whole body. Let it heal your heart, replenish your soul and support your spirit to move forward with love. Use this renewed energy to help you cherish your ambitions and make these desires reality.

Jade is the sacred stone of the New Zealand Maoris, who call it greenstone. Seen as a "dream stone," green jade can help encourage meaningful dreams. Position it on the forehead in meditation or before going to sleep to enable you to remember and understand the messages in your dreams, as well as release the suppressed emotions they represent.

Let this crystal remind you that we are all spiritual beings on a journey doing our best. Wear a green jade pendant every day to help you become more of who you really are, living from the heart, in each and every moment.

Peridot

BEST FOR:
Finding your purpose, attracting money, luck, peace and love, boosting well-being.

LOOKS:
Various shades of olive green, from light to the most prized dark olive green.

Our ancestors correctly believed that Peridot was brought to earth by an explosion of the sun, so carries the power of sunshine. The Ancient Greeks felt this gem exuded a vibration of royalty, bringing the wearer better health and increased wealth. They would carve the image of a torch onto a piece of peridot to encourage the manifestation of good fortune.

This crystal represents well-being and brings peace, warmth and radiance, reinvigorating mind and body to open up to new levels of awareness. It will connect you to divine consciousness, help you grow spiritually and realize your deeper purpose.

Meditate with peridot to bring understanding and insight into your self-sabotaging habits or the negative emotions holding you back. Stay connected to this crystal to realize your true worth, ultimate perfection and feel love, acceptance and gratitude—keys to manifesting the life you want.

Peridot powerfully generates the frequency of increase. Worn as jewelry, you can expect to manifest greater wealth, happiness and love in your life. Add it to a necklace as a pendant, and positive energy will flow from your heart space, increasing your awareness of love. If you wear peridot as a bracelet on your projective (right if you are right-handed) wrist, you'll easily share this loving energy with those around you. While having it on your receptive hand (the one you don't use that often—left if you're right-handed), you'll constantly be able to bring in more positivity, better health and increased prosperity.

Carry peridot in your pocket daily as a good-luck charm and to keep your energy high. At work or school, it can bring confidence in your talents, help you give an eloquent presentation and increase your profits. A protective stone, it will guard you from jealousy, deception and gossip.

It can give your love life a boost too—resolving heartbreak, releasing guilt or blame, and forgiving yourself and others, so you can move on in peace and happiness. It helps you feel content with your life, look inward for guidance and prize independence and acceptance.

Pyrite

BEST FOR:

Manifesting wealth, shifting from lack to abundance.

LOOKS:

Sparkly silvery gold, either in clusters or often in cubes.

Pyrite is famously called "Fool's Gold" after prospectors mistook it for real gold, long ago. It is actually a lighter color, harder and more brittle than real gold. Pyrite's shiny cubic composition will attract money to you when you work with it regularly.

Its name comes from the Greek word *pyr* or *pyros*, which means fire, because it creates sparks when struck with metal or stone. Consequently, it resonates with fire energy, bringing warmth, inspiration and confidence into your career and finances in particular. This stone awakens the inner warrior in us all, promoting strong will, focus and determination—needed to manifest the best in life.

This is a masculine stone of action and ambition, perfect for attracting more wealth and abundance. It connects with the solar plexus chakra and, when held there, sends a flood of power into this area to increase your zest for life. This helps you overcome any anxiety or destructive tendencies and build a solid foundation for new, more positive and productive habits to make you unstoppable in your achievements.

Work with pyrite in meditation as a mirror to yourself, letting it show you the causes behind, and solutions to, any feelings of unworthiness that will stop you from fully manifesting abundance. Hold some pyrite in your hand while looking at your reflection in a mirror. Gaze lovingly into your eyes and say, "I am worthy of success now."

Meditate with pyrite to stimulate your artistic energy and give you a creative edge if you work in the arts, architecture or sciences. Pyrite helps you commit to long-term projects, so it's an excellent stone for students to carry with them to their studies. It will also protect you from harm, especially if you're working or studying away from home.

Place a piece of pyrite where you work to bring high-frequency energy to the area, clearing stress caused by debts or working too hard. It will relieve mental confusion or fatigue and replace it with a clear head, renewed focus and enthusiasm. It can boost your leadership skills and give you the impetus to ask for and get a promotion. If you have a business card, place some pyrite on top of it to attract success and new career opportunities.

Rose Quartz

BEST FOR:
Manifesting unconditional love, romance and healing.

LOOKS:
Quartz with a rose-pink hue from traces of titanium, iron or manganese.

Rose quartz is known as "the love stone," and is said to have spread love, warmth and passion by legendary love god Cupid. This light-pink quartz brings peace and calm in relationships and melts away fear, resentment and anxiety, leaving you feeling carefree and open to love. The Egyptians believed in its healing abilities so much they carved rose quartz rocks into face masks believing it could clear the complexion and prevent the effects of aging.

Beads made of rose quartz have been found dating back to 7000BCE, from the civilization known as Mesopotamia, now Iraq.

Whether you want to increase your self-love, smooth over a family rift or bring a new lover into your life, rose quartz is a must-have crystal for your collection.

Thought to ease stress and induce rest, put a piece under your pillow at night, to help you get a good night's sleep and increase your love vibrations at the same time. Use it to open up your heart chakra and welcome love into your life. Lie down on your back in a comfortable place. Take a few deep breaths. Now place a small piece of rose quartz on the center of your chest, where your heart chakra sits. Breathe in its energy, imagining its soft pink hue filling your whole body with love. See this gentle pink energy of love clearing your heart chakra of any wounds from past relationships or your upbringing. Let it melt away any negativity from old partnership patterns. Keep breathing in that soothing, warm energy of love from the rose quartz as you go about your day.

Wear rose quartz as a pendant close to your heart chakra to open it up even more. Or carry a small tumbled rose quartz stone in your pocket all day to touch whenever you feel the need for some nurturing energy. Keep a chunk of rose quartz on your bedside table to keep the loving energy strong in your current relationship.

Set up a love altar in the love area of your home or bedroom to bring a loving relationship into your life. In feng shui, this is in the far right section of your room or floorplan. Place a rose quartz heart along with two red or pink candles to light daily, and meditate on true love coming into your life. Add other pairs of symbols of love—photos of happy couples or lovebirds—to the altar to boost your chances.

Tiger's Eye

BEST FOR:
Luck and bravery in new ventures, creative flow, willpower to stick with changes.

LOOKS:
Brown and golden silky stripes, in a "cat's-eye" effect.

Tiger's Eye is an ancient talisman said to bring good luck and great fortune. Ancient Egyptians believed it transmitted the power of the sun god Ra, while the Romans would carry this gem to battle to help them be brave. Thought to contain the power of not just the sun but the earth as well, tiger's eye helps transform pure energy into practical reality and tangible success.

It's a great stone to meditate with if you are planning a new project or taking up financial opportunities, as it will guide you to make balanced, rational decisions to bring success. Keep a piece of this crystal in your office or work area at home to manifest good fortune and attract a steady income, especially if you're an entrepreneur. It will help you stay focused on the task ahead and use your talents to maximum capability.

With its multi-dimensional access, tiger's eye can help if you need a fresh perspective, as it shows there are many ways to financial success.

Focusing on this gemstone will help you think outside the box and come up with interesting, creative solutions. If you have to present your ideas in a meeting, perform in public or take an exam, this bold gem will assist in overcoming any fears you have. It also brings wisdom to your spending, so when you manifest wealth you use it well.

If you want to manifest a healthier lifestyle, carry tiger's eye to boost your willpower and energy levels to help you stick with the changes you need to make. It is said to reduce cravings as well as feelings of inadequacy, and helps you persevere with the hard work of creating a healthy way of living.

Tiger's Eye can also help build better family relations. Having a prominent piece of it in the home will balance and soothe fraught relationships, encourage harmony and enable you to find common ground. It's one of the best gems to bring calm resolve to any crisis. Family counselors, professional mediators or anyone having to undertake tough negotiations should carry tiger's eye.

To make a prosperity charm with tiger's eye, keep a piece of it in a money pot and add a coin every day. Keep this pot in a warm spot to incubate wealth.

Titanium Rainbow Quartz

BEST FOR:
Awakening all chakras, creative expression, ultimate manifestation.

LOOKS:
Shimmery, rainbow-colored quartz.

Titanium Rainbow Quartz is quartz that has been specially bonded with titanium to give it its rainbow shimmer. This man-made gem is the most powerful of the coated quartz crystals, with titanium—otherwise known as the metal of power—greatly amplifying the effects of the "master healer" quartz. Consequently, this metallic stone is often called "the manifestation crystal."

This vibrant gem connects with, and energizes, the whole chakra system, sending Kundalini energy up the spine to boost your mood and help you realize and focus on what your soul needs for its evolution.

Creating a multi-dimensional shift in your life, it is said to awaken your innermost desires and parts of you formerly dormant so you can give more of your true self to the world. It will help you uncover your purpose, but if confusion or questions arise, wear titanium rainbow quartz around your neck in a pendant and the solutions will manifest.

With its rainbow shimmer symbolizing angelic guidance, wearing or carrying this stone will help you get in touch with this higher realm for inspiration and wisdom. This will heal your aura of any blockages holding you back from your full manifesting potential, and speed up whatever you want to come into being. As you connect with spiritual guidance more, meditating with this crystal will give you the confidence to communicate the messages you receive, and request back to the universe what it is you truly desire.

Also known as flame aura quartz, it can be an excellent muse, helping you find creative ways to express yourself. It will bring a sense of perfect timing to the things you say, and help you think clearly before speaking, so your words are taken in a positive way.

Place a cluster of titanium rainbow quartz on your desk at work for assistance when drafting emails or writing features or reports. If you have a novel in you, this crystal can help it manifest by inspiring you to get writing.

Let titanium rainbow quartz manifest more energy, humor and enjoyment in your life. This will enable you to relax and trust that your deepest dreams and desires will manifest into reality.

This gem is suitable for all astrological signs. It contains all the colors of the rainbow and stimulates all chakras.

Crystal recipes for manifesting

Here are some general tips on using crystals to manifest, plus specific combinations that work especially well.

✧ Choose any of the above crystals that resonate most with you or represent what you want to attract, and place them in a charm bag. Take your time holding and looking at each gem as you place it in the bag while stating its purpose or visualizing the outcome. Carry this charm bag with you to support you and bring your wishes to fruition.

✧ To manifest financial freedom and success, place a small bowl of money crystals from this section in the left-hand corner of your home or office as you stand from the front door. This is the money and career area according to feng shui. It should be free of clutter and contain pictures or ornaments that help you feel confident in your abilities and attract success.

✧ Add moldavite to titanium rainbow quartz for a power combo to transform you inside and out. Titanium quartz will have you pulsing with positivity, while moldavite will make you much more aware of the increased synchronicities that occur. They'll get you ready to act on them to move your life forward positively.

✧ To give your love life a lift, place crystals for manifesting love and romance, such as rose quartz, in the southwest corner of your home. Sleeping with some rose quartz under your bed or on your bedside table works in the same way to increase romance.

✧ Pair rose quartz with green aventurine to attract a new true love. Aphrodite, the goddess of love, is symbolized by rose quartz, while Tara, the goddess of the night, and Persephone, the spring goddess, add seduction and dynamism to green aventurine.

✧ Meditate with moonstone and rose quartz together, and they will align your chakras to make you positively glowing with divine charm, as well as awaken your intuition and make you aware of your deeper emotions, so you'll know if a new relationship is the one. This combination is also good for anyone in an established relationship, to keep it rooted in love.

✧ To manifest a family, place a rounded piece of amber with a pointed jet crystal in a red cloth bag tied with three knots of red ribbon. Put this fertility charm bag under the bed during lovemaking.

A crystal grid

Combining a few manifestation crystals in a grid makes them even more powerful, as their energies are combined with the sacred geometry of the formation you lay them out in, amplifying their ability to attract what you desire.

Print out or simply draw the seed of life geometry pattern representing the seven stages of creation. This sacred design represents the map to infinite possible paths and new beginnings, making it a great tool to focus your intention to manifest anything you want in your life. The symbol, combined with the crystals, will help you succeed at your goal in harmony, honesty and balance with your true intentions and what's ultimately right for you according to higher consciousness.

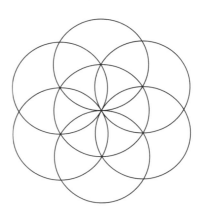

✧ First make sure the crystals you use have been cleansed and charged to connect with the energy of each other.

✧ Place strong amplifying and master attractor clear quartz in the center, then add these gems in positions that feel right to you.

✧ Iolite will reveal the mind and the heart's true desires, enhance your imagination to visualize what you want, and strongly attract your dream life to you.

✧ Some grounding and protective pyrite is good to have on your grid as a powerful crystal to manifest wealth.

✧ Add a piece of citrine to bring abundance and well-being.

✧ Good luck and prosperity gem jade needs to go on here, to gently open up your heart chakra to attract what your heart deeply desires.

As you're adding each crystal to the grid, really take the time to feel its frequency, and embed it with your intention to manifest a new lover, job or more money. Sit looking at the grid, and meditate on the crystals working to bring your desires to you at the right time. The most ideal time to create such a grid is a new moon; then, leave it out in your meditation area or on an altar for a lunar month to work its magic.

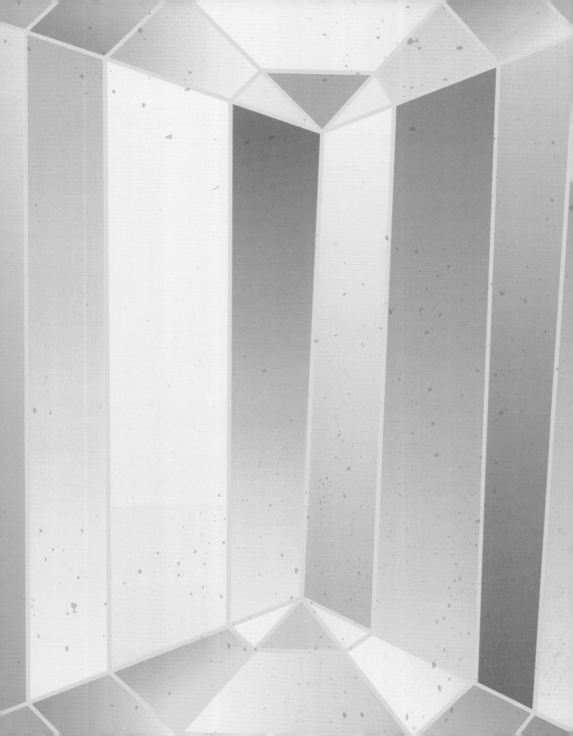

The Best Crystals For Your Home

Choose the right crystals for certain areas of your home and they will help protect you from harm, bring peace or energize where needed.

Crystals in the home

Having crystals in your home can only make you happier. Cleansed before use, programmed with conscious intention and positioned in the right place, they help in countless areas of your life.

Emotionally, they can clear the blockages and habits that are stopping you from living the life you want and deserve. Some, such as celestite and blue calcite, can lift your spirits, help you find your purpose, and get you to focus on making your goals a reality. Physically, gems can help calm you down, assist with healing, and block bad vibes. Spiritually, amethyst, peridot and clear quartz, among others, can enable you to meditate deeper, connect to higher dimensions and help you live in a new awakened, joyful way.

Certain crystals dotted around your home, workspace and yard will emit their energy into the areas they are positioned in. Blue lace agate is said to calm children, while a large piece of selenite in a house can generate a peaceful, positive atmosphere to smooth relationships. Other gems encourage organization, new romance, or help clear communication. They can also just make beautiful conversation pieces in the home, and can be dramatic additions to your decor.

A small bowl of your favorite crystals can keep the atmosphere in that room balanced and upbeat even if there's been drama, tension or change. It can encourage people to work together and not argue. Simple crystal tricks include keeping a piece of citrine in your wallet for increased wealth, or putting a piece of moss agate under your pet's

bed to help it settle down.

Gems will also work their magic according to feng shui, the ancient Chinese art of energy flow in the home. With this, your house or room is divided into different sections that reflect various areas of your life. For example, the left corner of your room is the career and wealth area, so you want gems such as citrine and jade there, creating dynamic and successful energy.

Crystals can also help our health by protecting us from the harmful effects of electromagnetic frequency and increased radiation from modern technology. Placing shungite, black tourmaline or smoky quartz between you and your device can soak up any potentially damaging energy.

Making crystal elixirs might work for you too. Simply leave your chosen crystal in a bottle of water in the fridge overnight to let its energies filter into the liquid. Then drink it when you need their energy, or make your guests cups of tea with it to pass on the good vibes.

In whatever way you want to use crystals in your home, surround yourself with the right amount. Choose intuitively, keep them cleansed, and ask them to work for you in the areas most needed.

Amber

BEST FOR:

Harmony and happiness in the home, attracting love, keeping calm.

LOOKS:

Mostly transparent golden, yellow or sometimes brown. Can contain fossilized insects or plants.

One of the world's oldest and most prized treasures, dating back between 30-60 million years in the Baltic, Amber is not actually a crystal but is fossilized resin from ancient coniferous trees. Because it sometimes contains plants or insects, it was said to contain the essence of life, and was seen as the stone of the mother goddess, connected to the sun and fire. It was used as a healing and protective amulet in Ancient Egypt, Cretan times (2000BCE), and the Middle Ages in Europe. Trade in this substance, reminiscent of the sun, created prehistoric trade routes in the world.

A protective charm, amber is a good gem to have in your home to attract prosperity as well as create an atmosphere of calm, cheerfulness and mutual respect. If it's new love you'd like in your life, wear it as a pendant. It connects with the solar plexus and sacral chakra to give you energy and motivation to act on your desires.

Brighten up your house with Amber's golden glow, and let its warm, sunny energy bring peace and stability to your home. It absorbs negative energy and transforms it into positive—and was once burned as incense for this purpose. A large piece of amber in the center of the room can dispel depression and anxiety, and boost self-worth so your inner radiance shines. Create a cozy cushioned area in your home where you can sit and look at a piece of glowing amber every day in winter to chase away seasonal affective disorder.

In a family home, Amber will help children relax, speak confidently and stay calm. It has been used for centuries to keep children from harm and ease teething pain. It also guards against conflict, again by taking the negative energy in the room and transforming it into positive.

Amber encourages the body to heal itself. Necessary in today's world, it can protect against electromagnetic pollution from technological gadgets, so place this crystal next to computers and phones. If you are sitting next to this substance while working, it will balance your own electromagnetic system and help get rid of headaches caused by stress.

Although usually golden orange, amber can also be blue, violet, green or black.

Black Obsidian

BEST FOR:

Protection, soaking up stress and negative vibes.

LOOKS:

Pure, glossy black or very dark brown.

Obsidian is made of earth, water and fire and formed from molten lava in the latter stages of volcanic eruptions. It was sharpened and used for tools and weapons as far back as 7,000 years ago. Obsidian is known as the mirror stone because it was once polished and used for mirrors and high-status decoration and scrying by the Mayans and other ancient civilizations. It's still a good tool for divination during meditation, as it can assist with seeing the future and contacting the spirit world.

Having obsidian in your home will make it a truly safe haven. Known as a "psychic vacuum cleaner," it clears negative energy from its environment. A protective stone, it will put up a barrier to burglaries or other unwanted guests, bullying from others, and psychic attack, enabling you to safely retreat from the world.

Its dark color is known to deepen your connection to the natural, physical world. Place a large piece on a table or wall in your yard or patio and allow obsidian to boost your strength and power, especially if you've felt drained or fearful about existence on earth during this tumultuous time.

Shiny black obsidian supports you in times of change, and blocks out everyday stresses and anxieties to help you relax. If you find you overspend, or overindulge in anything, an obsidian charm can boost self-control. However, it is also a powerful truth stone, and meditating with it will reveal your deepest insecurities and destructive patterns, which may not be easy to face, but when you're ready you can use black obsidian to help you heal your shadow side and become more balanced.

If you are finding obstacles to your career, place obsidian in the area of your home connected to career (the left-hand corner as you face inwards from the front door). A small sphere placed there, or a bowl of tumbled obsidian stones, will help rebalance your work energy, soak up stress, and inspire creativity so that your life can flow smoothly again.

Do not put obsidian on the floor, or anywhere it might get neglected, it needs to be regularly cleansed of all the negative energy it absorbs. Do this by placing it under any light source.

Blue Lace Agate

BEST FOR:
Creating a calm atmosphere, clear communication.

LOOKS:
Very pale blue with white or darker blue lines.

Blue lace agate, with its light-blue energy and slower frequency than many other crystals, will bring a calm, peaceful energy to any home. Sometimes associated with the Virgin Mary, and therefore motherhood, this gem nurtures and supports, soothes upset children, and helps healers increase their abilities.

Use this crystal at home or at work to diffuse anger and bring peace to any situation or gathering where there might be a clash of characters. Soak blue lace agate in bottles of water overnight to make an effective elixir for your family, friends or colleagues to drink. This will help avoid confrontations and ensure that criticism is expressed kindly.

Put some blue lace agate stones on your desk at work to transform any unhelpful, negative vibes with more uplifting, productive energy. Placed on a bedside table, the soothing, tranquil energy of blue lace agate will greatly relieve anxiety, stress or nervousness. It helps you find your voice and builds self-confidence to help you speak your truth with kindness. Wear it as a choker necklace to really work its magic on the throat chakra it corresponds with, opening and clearing it so your well-chosen words can flow freely.

Blue lace agate is also good for grounding and balancing the ups and the downs, the light and the dark, within us. If your siblings or children keep bickering, making you stressed and angry, light some blue candles surrounded by pieces of blue lace agate to bring serenity back to your home.

In feng shui, blue lace agate emits the still, strong and pure energy of water. This element brings rebirth and regeneration into your life. Add water's flowing and yielding yet powerful energies to the areas of your home where you feel it is most needed. Traditionally, the water element sits in the north of the home, the area associated with your life path and career. Place this crystal here and watch your career flow more smoothly. You can also put some of this crystal in the east side of your home for improved health, the southeast spot for abundance, and the southwest area to boost your love and marriage chances.

Celestite

BEST FOR:
Connecting to the angelic realm, calming atmospheres, soothing troubled relationships.

LOOKS:
Usually clusters and geodes of light blue, but can be found in white, orange, red and brown.

Celestite has a gentle, uplifting energy that cleanses its surrounding area, allowing you to relax and feel the presence of the celestial realm. This crystal will fill your home with a calm atmosphere, allowing divine energy to filter through, and helping you connect with angelic guides and your higher consciousness.

The soft energy emitted from celestite activates the throat, third eye and crown chakras, enabling you to develop your spiritual intuition easily. Lie in meditation, with pieces placed on these chakras, and you will find that you float into a deeper meditation effortlessly, picking up messages from spirit guides clearly. Fears and insecurities will disappear with this crystal in your home, as you realize you are safe and protected by your guides.

If a room in your home feels chaotic or full of emotional turbulence, place a piece of this light-blue crystal in a prominent place to create peaceful harmony. It brings back hope and optimism when you're grieving or sad, and encourages reconciliation, calm discussion and happier experiences in fraught relationships. Because of its ability to bring about tranquility, it's a perfect stone for the bedroom or meditation area, to enable you to smoothly drift into sleep or stillness of mind. It will help you with dream recall and even astral travel.

If you have children, place celestite in their bedrooms to help soothe any fears they may have, brought on by the darkness, and enable them to sleep more easily. This gem will also protect them with white light and bring their angel guides closer.

Placed in your workspace, celestite brings clarity of mind, focus and good fortune. Use this crystal here to help avoid stress and attract positive energies. It will stop you from feeling overwhelmed by a heavy workload, and help you feel restored after a long day. Artists, designers, musicians and anyone working in creative industries can benefit from celestite's inspirational boost. If you work giving readings or selling crystals, keep celestite with you all the time to maintain your spiritual connection, keep strong ethics and achieve prosperity.

The world's largest known geode, at over 30 feet wide, is made of celestite and was found on an island in Lake Erie. Discovered when making a well for a winery, the owner of the land has now converted it into a crystal cave for visitors.

Fluorite

BEST FOR:
Protection, organization, making progress.

LOOKS:
Comes in a variety of colors including green, blue, purple, clear and brown.

Fluorite is a highly protective crystal, both physically and on a psychic level. In the home it is highly effective at blocking harmful electromagnetic frequencies from computers and phones. This gem is a must to place on your desk and in your main living area. Create a protective fluorite grid around your computer, or place one between you and the tech that affects you in any way. In the right place, fluorite can combat effects of geopathic stress, coming from disrupted areas of the earth's magnetic field.

Meditate with it regularly and this gem will help you connect with your true self, enabling you to lose external influence. Fluorite stabilizes the aura, purifies negative energies, and clears stress, leaving you ready to go forward and make real progress.

It organizes everything from your body and mind to the clutter in your workspace and your relationships. In the living room, when free of external clutter, fluorite will encourage an uplifting atmosphere, making your gatherings go well and enhancing a sense of relaxation. Harmony and balance reign, especially if fluorite sits on a coffee table. People's negative opinions or other unwanted influences are deflected—it's a cloak around your aura.

Having fluorite in your home will bring structure to your daily life, help you learn and think quicker, as well as heighten spiritual and everyday awareness. If you work with a group, at work and especially in your home for healing circles, teaching sessions or meetings, yellow fluorite in the room will help bring unification. Encouraging a cooperative spirit, it may even make your family focus on a unified task that needs doing.

Green fluorite in particular works well in your yard, as it attracts butterflies. Meditate outside with it and you can tune into the nature spirits present. You can use this color of fluorite to heal damaged plants by charging it with that intention, holding it over the affected area and then placing it in the pot.

Blue fluorite in your home can calm or revitalize your energy, depending on what's needed. Try making an essence of it by leaving it in water overnight and spraying it into the room.

Energetically clear fluorite often, as it is such a protective crystal and soaks up a lot of negative energy. It likes to be placed in a stream or bowl of water overnight.

This crystal doesn't just work at home; you can keep its qualities working all day long by wearing fluorite earrings or holding and rubbing it as a palm stone.

Jet

BEST FOR:
Protection, absorbing negativity, grounding.

LOOKS:
Black like coal, but usually polished.

Jet is not a crystal but is, in fact, fossilized wood from antiquity. It's been found in graves for centuries. Used since the Bronze Age in jewelry and ornaments, the best was from northeast England, from where the Romans imported it to protect them from evil entities. From then on, it's been believed to protect from negative, draining energy, violence or illness.

Queen Victoria wore jet after the death of her husband, Prince Albert, as it was said to help with grief. If your home is full of sadness after trauma or the loss of a loved one, whether through death or divorce, place jet in the main living area. It helps you come to terms with a situation or relationship ending, so you can move on to the next phase of your life.

Jet will also alleviate anxiety and quash nightmares, so the children's bedrooms might need a jet crystal in them too. If your child has many worries, ask them to talk about them while holding the jet. Then bury the stone in your yard to take away their fears.

Place a piece of jet facing the front or back door to push bad vibes away. It will enable you to stay grounded and stabilize any area of your life, alleviate depression and help you let go of old emotions.

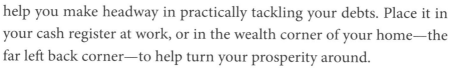

If you have money troubles, use jet to balance your finances and help you make headway in practically tackling your debts. Place it in your cash register at work, or in the wealth corner of your home—the far left back corner—to help turn your prosperity around.

If you're attracted to jet in a shop, you are likely to be an old soul, with many memories of past-life experiences. Meditate with it to help you access these, as jet acts as a gateway to the past and other dimensions for spiritual development. Jet links to the root chakra and awakens kundalini energy. Placed on your heart chakra when lying down in meditation, it will move that force up through all chakras to the crown, clearing your system inside and out.

If you've inherited jet jewelry that's been passed down for generations, make sure you cleanse it carefully before use, as it will have soaked up a lot of the previous wearers' energy. Bury jet in soil overnight to release it from the energy of others.

Jet is a purifier of all other stones. Simply place your crystals with jet in a bowl and leave them overnight.

Moss Agate

BEST FOR:
New beginnings, connecting with nature, calming animals.

LOOKS:
Milky white or translucent, with tendrils of manganese or iron that have made patterns like moss or lichen. Sometimes they can be dark green with blue inclusions.

With plant matter inside it, moss agate is often known as "the gardener's stone," as it encourages plant growth and agriculture. Many ancient cultures revered moss agate as a stone for good fortune, including Native Americans, who used it to bring rain. Europeans offered it to the spiritual guardians of the land in orchards, fields and gardens to get a good yield.

Plant this crystal with your plants, in a pot or flowerbed, to ensure that they stay healthy and abundant. Moss agate can help you communicate with nature spirits and devas who can assist with the success of your crops. A nurturing stone to encourage patience, peace and stability from the highs and lows of life, moss agate helps bring calm, especially when placed in your living area. It aids resilience, improves the positive parts of people's personalities, and helps everyone get along better. It is a wonderful crystal to place in the bedroom or meditation corner to help you quietly contemplate your spiritual growth and the interconnectedness of life.

According to feng shui, moss agate brings wood energy into your home, attracting good health, vitality and strength, especially for any new endeavors such as children or creative projects. Have one on the dinner table to boost nourishment from meals. Add one to your child's collection to ensure that they grow healthily. If you're starting a new project at work, place one on your desk to help it grow.

At work, moss agate in your office will slowly attract a promotion or raise. It especially boosts new businesses and is your talisman if you're self-employed. Keep a piece close by if doing your accounts or tax returns, and it will also help you save.

Moss agate helps pets, too. If they're overactive, nervous or aggressive, you can place a small stone under their bed to calm them down—this works especially well with animals from rescue centers. If you live in a city, moss agate in your cat's bed will restore their connection with nature. Moss agate can help the bond between children and pets, balancing both their energies in a positive way.

Depictions of the Virgin Mary, Jesus, John the Baptist, angels and various other human forms have manifested themselves in moss agate stones and can be found in churches and museums around the world.

Shungite

BEST FOR:
Grounding, healing and protecting from radiation and electromagnetic smog.

LOOKS:
Black, oily or dull-looking; or elite shungite, which has a silvery tint to it and sometimes gold inclusions.

Although shungite has been on the planet for at least two million years, its use in homes around the world is relatively recent. Its carbon mineral makeup contains fullerenes, which conduct electricity yet shield from electromagnetic frequency and radiation from modern technology. Fullerenes contain powerful antioxidants that absorb and eliminate harm in our environment and from our bodies. Research on fullerenes won three scientists the Nobel Prize in chemistry in 1996.

Historically, water infused with shungite was drunk to promote healing. Russian czar Peter the Great is said to have visited the region where shungite was discovered, and used the power-packed water for its beneficial properties.

Soak a chunk of the duller shungite in a bottle of water overnight to purify the water and fill it with the mineral's healing antioxidants to boost your immune system and general well-being. Drinking this two or three times a day will help detoxify the body of any pollutants and maintain healthy cell growth. Testing has also revealed shungite to be able to absorb pesticides, free radicals and bacteria from the body. It can even prevent and lessen the symptoms of colds.

Shungite is a must for your home; reduce electromagnetic radiation by placing stones or pyramids of it at the base of devices such as your cell phone, laptop or wifi router. You can even get shungite discs to stick on the back of your phone to soak up the potentially damaging EMF rays. Carry one with you if you're traveling through airports, to protect you from the energy emitted by security scanners.

Shungite activates all the chakras, boosting energy and clearing the mind of all negativity. If your emotions are up and down, or you worry a lot, meditating with shungite in your hand allows light to fill your body and your aura, keeping anxiety, depression and external negative energy at bay.

If you suffer from insomnia or tension headaches, try placing a shungite sphere or pyramid by your bed to combat the effects of stress. It's a good grounding stone, so it's worth placing in your yard, and sitting or lying on the ground and meditating while holding it, to give your body a stronger, healing connection to the earth.

You can now get shungite paint for the walls of your house to protect against electromagnetic frequency coming from outside sources, such as smart meters, solar panels and street lights.

Smoky Quartz

BEST FOR:
Grounding, protecting, dispelling negative energy.

LOOKS:
Translucent quartz turning gray, smoky, yellowish, brown or black.

Originally called morion when it was discovered and used by the Druids and Celts around 300BCE, smoky quartz is the national gem of Scotland. Here it became common in Highlander adornment, and is one of the power stones on the handle of the Scottish dagger, which is still part of the country's national costume.

Smoky quartz is exceptional at clearing negative energies, grounding your physical body, and eliminating stress. Place one in your bedroom if you have trouble sleeping to stop your mind from racing and help you drift off into a deep slumber.

It's another good stone to use to block geopathic and electromagnetic waves that can harm the body. Place it by your cordless phone or above disturbed ley lines to stop their energy from affecting you. Or sit holding this crystal when you feel overloaded by "electrosmog."

Linking with the root chakra, this powerful crystal will increase your connection to the earth, inspiring environmental concern and pride at being incarnated in human form at this time. It brings strength and stability as well as protection from psychic attack or emotional and physical stress. Stand in your yard, on the grass, with your smoky quartz in your receptive hand pointing downwards, and feel any negativity drain out of you and into the earth.

This crystal also protects your home, workplace or vehicle from theft or damage by others. Add a small stone to your wallet, bag or glove compartment of your car to ensure safety. In your car, smoky quartz is also thought to protect against road rage, mechanical breakdowns and other driving dangers.

Use smoky quartz in all the main areas of your house to counter bad moods or nasty comments that bring you down. Let its energy lift depression, promote positive thoughts and bring passion and vitality into your life.

If bullying or gossip occurs in the workplace, lay dark smoky quartz pointing outwards on your desk in a semi-circle to help you stay calm and concentrate on getting the job done. Wear it as a pendant to boost your survival instincts and help your career goals manifest. If you need to stay rational, get organized or focus on any calculations, place this crystal near you to help. You may see more psychic phenomena such as ghosts, spirit guides or UFOs when wearing or carrying smoky quartz, as it draws these into your auric field to make them easier for you to perceive.

Turquoise

BEST FOR:

Leadership qualities, clear communication, prosperity and success.

LOOKS:

Turquoise copper aluminum material, with greenish speckles of iron.

Turquoise is one of the oldest stones used by humans, with beads dating back to 5000BCE found in Iran. In Ancient Egypt, where it was mined in 3200BCE, Hathor, the goddess of love, marriage, music and women, was known as the Lady of Turquoise. In many Native American cultures, it was seen as a male power stone that only warriors were allowed to wear. In Mexican ruins, 9,000 turquoise beads were found in a single warrior chief's grave.

At home, turquoise brings both male and female energies into balance, enhancing communication between the sexes, bringing empathy, creativity and inner calm along with strength, ambition and alertness. It stimulates romantic love and works to create a restorative atmosphere encouraging well-being, success and good luck. Rest while holding turquoise if you're feeling exhausted, panicky or down in any way, and let it lift your low mood. A purification stone,

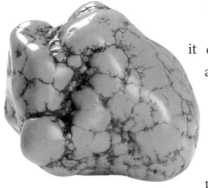

it clears negativity from the mind, and also electromagnetic smog from your external surroundings.

Turquoise is sometimes called "the campaigner's stone" because it will bring strength and leadership to those protecting the environment or taking peaceful action to protect human rights. Wearing it as a necklace will help calm your nerves if you have to speak in public. Working on balancing the throat chakra, it helps you express yourself effectively and clearly communicate any repressed feelings that may be holding you back from your true potential.

At work, keep turquoise with financial documents or accounts to attract wealth by making shrewd investments. Wearing it can lead to promotion or increased travel for work—and it will also protect your possessions from theft. It's a useful crystal for many professions: accountants, and anyone using computers, can use turquoise to help relax their minds; it helps cure writer's block and ease performance anxiety in anyone working in television or radio; and laborers should carry it to protect them from physical injury.

Traditionally, turquoise was braided into a horse's mane to stop it from stumbling. At home, if you place a piece of turquoise near stairs, it can prevent falling, especially in children or the elderly. Children can carry this stone to combat shyness and stop bullying. A pet with a piece of turquoise attached to its collar will not get lost or stolen. Turquoise should ideally be given as a gift, not bought for oneself.

Household problem = crystal solution

For most household problems, there's a crystal that can help.

MESSY, CHAOTIC HOUSE

Fluorite organizes inside and out to bring harmony and structure to you daily life and help clear your clutter.

PEOPLE ARGUING AND NOT GETTING ALONG

Blue lace agate on your coffee table or dining table should ease conversations and stop anyone from saying anything they might regret. Place a large piece of amber in your living space to guard against conflict, transform negative vibes into positive, and dispel any sadness or anxiety.

NOISY NEIGHBORS

Put rose quartz next to the wall between you and your angry neighbors to calm their shouting and promote peace.

HYPERACTIVE CHILDREN OR PETS

Purple fluorite helps dogs behave better when they're outdoors, and helps children calm down, while moss agate balances both when placed in their beds.

UNHELPFUL TEENAGERS

Place amazonite in their bedroom to help them get out of bed at a reasonable time and live a healthier lifestyle.

Ametrine will do the same, and will keep teens out of trouble.

ALLEVIATING NIGHTMARES

A piece of jet in the room or held in the hand to soothe someone before bed works wonders to quash bad dreams.

PLANTS KEEP DYING

If your plants are affected by central heating and look like they're wilting, place moss agate crystals in the soil.

Fluorite can mend damaged plants; simply pass it over the affected area, then bury the stone in the pot.

TECHNOLOGY MAKING YOU LETHARGIC AND SICK

If you're affected by electromagnetic frequency, wear shungite or stick a disc of it to the back of your cell phone.

You can also create a special grid of protection with shungite, black tourmaline or smoky quartz by placing small pieces of it in the corner of each room in your home to transform negative energies. Try joining the crystals in your mind, or using a quartz wand to protect your entire home.

Key crystals for each area

AT THE FRONT DOOR

✧ This is a key place to put crystals to keep away any unwanted visitors and attract good vibes only. To protect the whole home from harmful energies, place smoky quartz, black tourmaline or jet in the doorway.

✧ To attract only good vibes, place carnelian just inside the front door; if it's abundance you're after, use citrine.

LIVING ROOM

✧ A large piece of rose quartz or jade in your living space will bring love and harmony throughout the whole home.

✧ Place a wand of selenite on the coffee table to fill the place with positive light.

✧ Tiger's eye placed in a prominent position will help bring harmony to any turbulent family relationships.

✧ Labradorite will inject some fun into your home if you've been stuck in a rut.

DINING ROOM

✧ Amber or carnelian on the dining table will help stimulate healthy appetites.

✧ Citrine in the center of the room is said to keep conversation positive while you eat, as well as assisting with digestion.

✧ Orange calcite will create lively debate while keeping it upbeat and respectful.

KITCHEN

✧ To stimulate creative, confident cooking with ease, choose carnelian for kitchen surfaces.

✧ Red jasper is also energizing, and will wake you up in the morning as you make breakfast.

BEDROOM

FOR DEEP SLEEP

✧ Either sleep with a small smooth stone of amethyst or moonstone under your pillow or bed, or place a piece of rose quartz on your bedside table. Alternatively, soak an amethyst in water overnight and drink it before bedtime.

BETTER LOVE LIFE

✧ Turquoise balances the sexes and stimulates romantic love. If you want

to bring creativity and calm, along with strength and alertness into the bedroom, place a piece of turquoise on both sides of the bed.

OFFICE

TO COMBAT STRESS

✧ A black obsidian sphere or a dish of smaller tumbled stones will rebalance your workload.

FOR CREATIVITY

✧ Place clear quartz on your desk to ignite creativity, but balance it with lapis lazuli so you don't work too late into the night.

FOR CREATIVITY AND GOOD FORTUNE

✧ Celestite on your desk will get your creative juices flowing and ease stress.

FOR WEALTH AND ABUNDANCE

✧ Citrine in your wallet, on your financial documents, and in the career area (far left corner from the door) will attract success. Turquoise will also have this effect.

BATHROOM

✧ Have a dish of your favorite crystals here to add to bathwater for a boost. Jade will restore your tired body, rose quartz soothes frayed nerves, clear quartz added to your bath will energize, and turquoise will bring inspired ideas while you soak.

GARDEN

✧ Green aventurine helps plant roots fill with energy, and boosts plant growth, as does moss agate planted with your crops.

✧ Charge a clear quartz with your intention to grow a beautiful garden, or a reminder to water your plants regularly, and place the crystal in your outside space to work its magic.

Which crystal for which zodiac sign?

E ach zodiac sign has a few crystals that work best with it, because they either emanate a similar energy, or give your astrological personality a boost. Choose gifts for yourself, family and friends from the appropriate gems to boost your astrological traits as you wear them as jewelry or place them in prominent positions in your home to let their planetary influence fill your rooms.

ARIES
March 21—April 20
Diamond, bloodstone,
pyrite, hematite, jasper

GEMINI
May 22—June 21
Citrine, white sapphire,
ametrine, green aventurine

TAURUS
April 21—May 21
Rose quartz, emerald,
peridot

CANCER
June 22—July 22
Moonstone, pearl, selenite,
sodalite

LEO

July 23—August 23

Carnelian, topaz, tiger's eye, amber, clear quartz

SAGITTARIUS

November 23—December 21

Turquoise, ruby, azurite, rhodochrosite, iolite

VIRGO

August 24—September 22

Moss agate, blue sapphire, amazonite, yellow aragonite

CAPRICORN

December 22—January 20

Black onyx, garnet, jet, smoky quartz

LIBRA

September 23—October 23

Opal, lapis lazuli, celestite, rose quartz

AQUARIUS

January 21—February 18

Amethyst, sugilite, blue lace agate, angelite, moldavite

SCORPIO

24 October—November 22

Black obsidian, apache tear, coral, labradorite, malachite

PISCES

February 19—March 20

Jade, aquamarine, purple fluorite, kyanite

The Crystals That Are Best For Healing

Connect with certain crystals often to create a nourishing, holistic healing practice for yourself and to help you heal others, including your pets and the planet.

Healing with crystals

For centuries, crystals have been used for healing by expert practitioners and ordinary men and women wanting a gentle yet effective way to boost health and well-being. The right gems used in the right way can alleviate physical symptoms such as headaches, itchy skin and an upset stomach, and deeper emotional wounds, including post-traumatic stress or heartbreak, and mental anguish holding you back. They can give you a general energy increase, protect you from harmful electromagnetic frequency from electronic devices and ease the effects of arthritis, menopause or diabetes. Once you've figured out which crystals work best with your energy or ailment, there are various ways you can use them to holistically heal yourself and others.

The following ten crystals are some of the main ones for healing specific things. If you're just starting out, you can also use amethyst, citrine, rose quartz or clear quartz as powerful general healers of auras, emotions and atmosphere.

HOW CRYSTALS HEAL

Crystals emit a certain energy according to what they're made of, their color, and what they've been programmed to do by your focused attention. They work by vibrating a frequency that influences the mind, body and spirit, through your senses, your aura and your home.

Some crystals contain minerals widely known to help balance the body. Malachite, for example, contains copper, which is used to reduce inflammation and prevent swelling. These can be worn on the body, or carried in a pouch or in your pocket. Some can even be drunk as a specially made elixir (except for malachite, which can be toxic).

MAKING A CRYSTAL ELIXIR

Many crystals can be made into an elixir to boost health simply by placing a piece of the gem in a glass bottle of distilled or pure mineral water overnight. This can then be drunk to get the crystal benefits into the body, or heated and used as a topical solution for skin problems that the crystal might help with.

CLEARING AND ACTIVATING THE CHAKRAS

Other stones work on cleansing or stimulating the chakras when placed above their location on the body. This keeps the energy within you and your aura sparkling and working well. It also activates the areas of your psyche connected to them. For example, self-love is connected to the heart chakra, and confidence is linked to the solar plexus.

See page 35 for which crystals to use for which chakras. Then place the correct ones down the center of the body—yours or whoever you are giving a healing to—while lying down in meditation.

Relax for 20-30 minutes to let the crystals' energy take effect on the chakras beneath them, cleansing, balancing and energizing your whole system.

DIFFERENT WAYS TO HEAL

Other ways to absorb crystal energy include sleeping with a specific stone under your pillow or creating a healing grid of the crystals in the room where you want it to have an effect. You can also add crystals to your bathwater, to soak in their power.

Use your intuition and discernment to guide you in choosing the right crystal and where to place it. If there's a specific physical ailment you or someone else wants help with, simply place a small stone on the area, or hold it close to it for as long as you can, imagining its healing energy working its way to the problem.

HEALING YOURSELF

Before you start any healing, you may want to ask for support and protection from divine sources, such as the angels, a healing god or goddess, or your higher consciousness to work through you for the highest good. Hold your crystal in your hands and place it to your heart, filling it with love and asking that it do what's best for you or your patient.

Through meditation, by holding the healing crystal in your hands, you can absorb its powerful energy. Sit quietly and take some deep breaths. When you exhale, let out all negative thoughts and feelings.

As you breathe in, imagine the crystal's positive light filling your whole body. Visualize this energy as a soothing, warm liquid radiating from your heart to fill you up, expanding out into your aura as well. Sit peacefully feeling your crystal's energy making you whole and happy.

Once a week, you could try sitting inside a circle of different colored crystals laid out on the floor. See each of the rainbow of colors coming into your aura and being absorbed by your body for a full top-up of their energy. Red crystals will energize you, green will nurture you, and orange boosts creativity. Pink will fill you with love, blue helps clear communication, and purple links to higher realms. Afterwards, make sure you ground yourself and ask for protection from a black crystal such as jet or obsidian.

Alternatively, lie down comfortably and position the different colored crystals on top of their corresponding chakras for a complete cleansing of your whole mind, body and spirit as you rest.

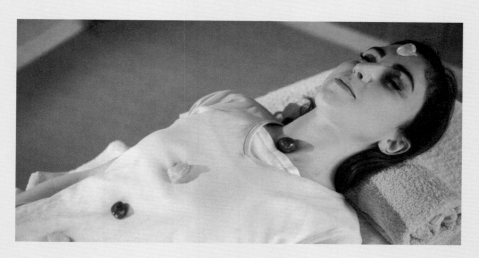

HEALING OTHERS

Contact healing is when the person being healed is present at the session. It doesn't mean you make contact with the crystal and their body. Usually the gem is held a couple of inches above the patient's body, always fully clothed. Listen to your intuition and sense the energy of the crystal regarding where it wants to be positioned and for how long. You may want to hold it in a certain area or move it gently and continuously over your patient.

When completed, always say a few words of thanks to your higher power and the crystal for its work. Remember to cleanse it well after every healing session if it absorbs energy.

DISTANT HEALING

You can also use crystals to send healing energy to people, groups or animals, as well as the oceans, earth or specific areas of the world that need help. Choose green or brown crystals, such as moss agate or jade, to heal the land or forests and the creatures that dwell there. Blue gems, including aquamarine or blue coral, work wonders on the waters of the world and the fish that swim in them. Tiger's eye or leopardskin jasper help endangered species stay healthy and strong.

Hold a larger crystal in your hands. Focus on filling the stone with prayers and intentions to heal whatever you've chosen to help. Say your wish out loud repeatedly into the crystal, or chant a healing mantra for it to absorb.

Inhale deeply and imagine the light from the crystal filling you up. Exhale any darkness. Continue to breathe in light until you are full of sparkling positive healing energy. Then send this healing light to your chosen subject as you breathe out, still saying the healing prayer or mantra in your mind. Visualize the healing taking place, and the person, pet or area shining with health and vitality.

You could also place the charged crystal on a photo of the absent friend, animal or place to be healed, and leave it there for as long as you want it to work its magic.

Amazonite

BEST FOR:
Soothing and communicating emotions rationally, encouraging a healthy lifestyle, blocking microwaves.

LOOKS:
Blue-green or turquoise opaque, sometimes darker green with white lines.

Amazonite has been used for healing and good fortune for centuries. It is believed to have featured on the breastplates of warrior women in the matriarchal Bronze Age tribe of Amazonians. Easy to carve, amazonite was made into beads and other jewelry by the early Mesopotamians, and into a scarab ring in King Tutankhamen's tomb. Found growing in slabs, the ancient Egyptian *Book of the Dead* was carved into it.

A crystal of courage and truth, it helps you bravely communicate what is true for you, and know and state your boundaries clearly. Often called the "peacemaker" stone, it enables you to see another viewpoint and, when placed in a room, will emanate peaceful vibes for reconciliation and healing. It can help you rectify inner conflicts.

Amazonite connects to and rebalances the heart and throat chakras, soothing turbulent emotions and assisting with honest, heartfelt communication. If you need to have a difficult conversation, put some amazonite in your pocket and let it help your words flow with compassion and kindness.

When self-healing with crystals, place a piece of amazonite on your throat to fully awaken this chakra and help this area of your body function better. Drink its essence in water to boost calcium intake and ease muscle spasms. Amazonite calms the nervous system, supports the thyroid gland, and encourages both men and women to live a healthy lifestyle.

Used often, amazonite will bring the masculine and feminine sides of your personality into balance—and in the workplace it is thought to combat sexism. It also harmonizes your intuition with your intellect, helping you feel what you need to do in the world and then bravely go and do it. If you have something you'd like to manifest, state it clearly to your amazonite and meditate with it often to activate your intention.

Amazonite is a powerful crystal to block electromagnetic emanations from your cell phone or computer; stick some to your phone or position it between you and the devices you use. Placed on your desk, it will bring focus to your purpose and success in your endeavors. In the kitchen, it will block microwave harm from gadgets as well as encourage other family members to help with household jobs.

Cleanse amazonite with a mint infusion to recharge its considerable powers.

Aquamarine

BEST FOR:

Water healing, increased intuition, clearing the throat chakra.

LOOKS:

Very light blue, clear to opaque.

This crystal-clear blue type of beryl was believed to be mermaids' treasure in ancient times. It was called "water of the sea" by Roman fishermen, who carried it with them for courage and safety on the oceans. It was also used by physicians to aid digestion and decrease fluid retention. Roman craftsmen made goblets from it to purify water.

Still believed to be purifying, you can make an aquamarine detox elixir to cleanse the body. Soak a stone in water overnight and drink it to soothe stomach pains, boost the immune and lymphatic systems, and clear the throat of infections or soreness. Soothing for tired or irritated eyes, it is even believed to help vision. Place a small, smooth tumbled stone on the eyelids for 20 minutes each night while you relax and let its cooling, calming properties take effect.

Aquamarine is one of the most powerful crystals for activating and clearing the throat chakra, helping you express yourself honestly with an open heart and greater confidence. Having it in your home will harmonize the atmosphere and keep angry emotions at bay, as well as assist in clearing out clutter mentally, emotionally and physically.

Meditating with it will bring acceptance of your true self, a deeper wisdom, and enable you to let go of built-up emotions. It's a lovely stone to receive courage and healing from if you're suffering from grief or going through major changes.

A powerful stone to boost psychic and spiritual development, use aquamarine to send absent healing to others. Place it on a photo of the person you want to help and imagine aquamarine's healing energy filling their body, aligning their chakras and bringing them back to full health.

You can also charge it with prayers to clean the oceans and protect all sea creatures, as it is especially linked with whales and dolphins. Place a piece of aquamarine on a picture of any endangered ocean life while seeing them thriving for decades to come. Feel the sparkling health of the waters of the world in your heart and let that energy ripple out around the planet. Closer to home, add some to your fish tank or pond to keep the marine creatures healthy.

With its gentle, compassionate energy, aquamarine encourages compromise, negotiation and service. It helps you take responsibility for yourself and others less fortunate, and assists humanity to become more healing, bringing natural justice and balance to our destructive and damaging habits.

Cleanse aquamarine in a blue glass bowl of seawater or salted mineral water on the night of a full moon, rinsing with pure water afterwards.

Aragon Star Clusters

BEST FOR:
Earth healing, grounding, stress relief.

LOOKS:
Mainly orange, gold and brown "sputnik" clusters, but also found in white, yellow, green and blue.

Aragonite is mostly found in spiky cluster formations of tube-shaped crystals exploding from a central point. Named after the Aragon River in Spain, where it was discovered in 1790, aragonite is a great grounding stone to bring you back into balance after stressful episodes. Balancing the heart and mind, it will help you stop focusing negatively on difficult situations and bring renewed strength and faith in your ability to meet any challenge.

A stone to encourage new beginnings, aragonite brings

stability, discipline and a pragmatic way of doing things, as well as a clearer mind and motivation. With aragonite in your home, family members might get better at timekeeping and tackle those chores today rather than next week!

Meditating with an aragonite cluster regularly will help you nourish yourself physically (by eating healthy regular meals) and emotionally (by taking time out to calm frayed nerves). It's a good gem to use to prepare for meditation because it raises your vibrations to a higher level spiritually and gives the body a boost of vitality.

Healers benefit from starting any session of healing by tuning into aragonite's energy to center themselves before working on others. Have aragonite around if you're going to do any smudging or dowsing to link strongly into the Earth Goddess energy to support you.

This crystal activates the root chakra and the earth chakra below our feet, deeply connecting us to mother earth. Feeling the ground beneath you while standing holding an aragonite star cluster will help you discern what healing the planet needs, and how to get it to it. If you suddenly feel an urge to ditch plastic, or plant trees everywhere you go, that's the effect of aragonite in your life.

With strong powers to heal the planet, it's no surprise that aragonite can clear geopathic stress or blocked ley lines. To do this, either place the stone on a map over the area you wish to send healing energy to, or, if you're able to visit, perform a healing ceremony, cleansing the crystal, programming it with prayers, and then planting it the soil.

To cleanse, bury aragonite in a pot of soil for a full day and night.

Blue Kyanite

BEST FOR:
Connecting with and healing the animal kingdom, attuning to the spirit world, increasing telepathy.

LOOKS:
Shards or blades of blue-white, opaque with a pearly sheen or transparent.

Blue kyanite is a fairly new crystal for healing and other spiritual work, found abundantly in Brazil. It's a powerful stone for connecting and attuning with animals of all kinds, plants and humans. It quickly calms the mind and body, allowing you to go deep into meditation, attuning swiftly with spirit guides, psychic powers and your own intuition.

This blue crystal stimulates the third eye and throat chakras, boosting your communication skills and self-expression while linking that with your deepest truth and higher guidance. It's also a great gem for aligning all chakras to clear your body's pathways for better healing, and attunement to the spiritual realm for help.

Use blue kyanite when performing healing to create a stronger link between you and the person or creature being healed. Work with it to send or receive healing energy and boost telepathy with friends, family

and pets. In meditation, hold a shard close to your third eye and tune in to a particular person to sense how they are feeling and what they need to help them in any way, or conjure up a positive healing image in your mind and send it to them. It can also assist you in astral travel or lucid dreaming—place it on your third eye when lying down before going to sleep.

Blades of blue kyanite make excellent wands to brush away any negative energy from others, dispelling anger, frustration and illusion. They make a soothing gift for anyone passing away to help them ground spiritual energy into their body so they can transition into the spirit world more smoothly.

Make a healing grid of blue kyanite to help you stop any self-destructive behavior patterns or if you feel you've moved away from your true path. Place rows of small kyanite shards coming out in six different directions from a central kyanite stone and meditate with this layout every night until you regain clarity. Lowering your gaze to just focus on the crystals, allow your mind to wander, allowing images and ideas to take form as they arise, bringing you insight, guidance and aligning you to your highest frequency again.

Kyanite does not absorb negative energy, so it never needs to be cleansed, but you can rejuvenate it by leaving it near plants first thing in the morning.

Carnelian

BEST FOR:
Healing from abuse, trusting yourself, and rejuvenating your relationships.

LOOKS:
Bright orange to red, semi-translucent glassy pebble, often containing lighter or darker spots and streaks.

The Latin root for this crystal's name means "flesh," and carnelian can certainly give your body a boost. Expect better health and vitality, plus increased metabolism and sex drive, when working with this vibrant orange or red stone of confidence and courage. Ancient warriors wore it around their necks to make them bold in battle, and it has long been believed to bring shy people out of their shells.

Carnelian is a very healing stone: it gives you energy, passion and motivation, as well as bringing abundance in all areas of your life. It is also believed to help the body heal after injury, whether physical or emotional, and it's well known for healing after abuse. It enables you to trust yourself and your perceptions again so that you can take the lead in your own joyful and fulfilling life.

As well as increasing creativity and concentration, it also rejuvenates relationships. Place a piece of carnelian under the corners of your mattress to bring passion and stamina back to the bedroom. Stimulating the lower three chakras, but especially the root chakra, it will boost libido and fertility, alleviate sexual anxieties, and ease menstrual or menopausal symptoms. Place a piece of carnelian on the skin at the solar plexus while lying down in meditation, and allow its surge of energy to work from that chakra down, balancing and grounding you as well.

Carnelian connects you more to your inner self while anchoring you in present reality. This, in turn, supports you to detox and heal from addiction to substances, especially any related to low self-esteem. Working with this gem will bring acceptance of life as well as less fear of death. It is beneficial for the elderly to carry carnelian in their pockets to lift the mood, and for men going through a mid-life crisis.

Honour this crystal's love of community spirit to gather with like-minded friends to use carnelian to send healing to ancient sacred sites or derelict buildings to preserve them. Ask a carnelian stone to heal the environment around it, then bury it in the earth. Or make an essence of carnelian with water and pour this onto the affected area.

If you have a bowl of gems in your home, add carnelian to it, as it cleanses other crystals.

Hematite

BEST FOR:
Grounding and balancing, cleansing
the blood, healing the spine.

LOOKS:
Metallic gray heavy
iron oxide, sometimes
found in brown-red
shades. Forms in rough
rosettes but more often
found smoothed shiny.

Hematite is iron oxide found commonly in iron ore all over the world. It also forms in quartz. Although mostly a metallic gray, some hematite has reddish brown streaks and marks in red when rough-cut and rubbed against another stone. Its name comes from the Greek word for blood, due to its color when ground into a powder.

So it's no surprise that hematite helps heal your blood, by cleansing it, stimulating iron absorption and boosting circulation, even easing heavy menstruation and bringing down blood pressure. Believed to regenerate tissue and help make red blood cells, it can also draw heat out of your body and be drunk as an elixir or placed on the forehead to soothe fevers.

An incredible stone for self-healing, hematite can actually pull out pain. Lie comfortably and hold a piece of hematite over the pain or the solar plexus chakra, and allow it to draw the ill feeling away.

Hematite has a strong grounding ability, pulling the root chakra down to the earth to align and balance you, making it useful for balancing emotions and aligning your spine.

Ask a friend to help with this healing: lie down on your front and have them place a piece of hematite at the top of your spine, one at the bottom and one on the problematic area. Relax with your head to one side and visualize your back fully healed. This eases the way for realignment and grounds your energy through your spine. Just don't lie like this for very long or if inflammation is present.

With its high iron content, hematite has a magnetic pull, which can attract the right opportunities to turn your dreams into reality. If worked with regularly, it can restore harmony to the body, focus the mind on figuring out practical problems, and enhance willpower and tenacity. Hematite is also known as the lawyer's stone, because it helps justice prevail in legal wrangles or neighborly disputes.

Spiritually, it was used for divination and polished into mirrors to deflect negativity in ancient times. Hematite is one to have on your meditation altar to stop negative energies entering your aura, especially during astral travel, which it stimulates.

Carry hematite with you during and after flying, as its power is said to combat jet lag.

Malachite

BEST FOR:
Purifying, protection and transforming negative energies to positive.

LOOKS:
Rich, vibrant green with swirling and eye-shaped darker or lighter green bands.

Raw malachite can be toxic, and should never be used by children or with animals, but in its more common, polished form it has been used for healing for centuries. Mined as long ago as 4000BCE, malachite was used in Ancient Egypt as a power stone to channel higher energy to earth. To help pharaohs be wiser leaders, they lined their headdresses with it. Malachite was also ground into a powder eyeshadow believed to enhance vision and spiritual insight.

A powerful protection stone since the Middle Ages, when it was thought to shield people from the "evil eye," malachite absorbs negative energy and pollutants from the environment and the body. It soaks up radiation and plutonium damage, and clears electromagnetic pollution when placed near televisions, computers, microwaves and other technology that emits harmful rays. Place at least two crystals in each room with any gadgets or fluorescent lighting in to combat toxic effects. Carry a small, smooth stone with you when on a plane to counteract radiation from flying.

Malachite draws out impurities, pain and inflammation from the body if placed carefully over the affected area, with a small cloth underneath. Lie down with a piece on your abdomen to relieve menstrual cramps or a stomach ache, or place on the jaw to ease a toothache. This healing gem is also believed to boost the immune system and circulation, stimulate cell regeneration and liver function and lower blood pressure. Worn around the waist, it is believed to help keep diabetes at bay (but it should never replace the advice of your doctor!). Many believe that malachite is still evolving, and will become one of the most important healing stones of the future.

A stone of transformation, it encourages deep emotional healing when placed on the solar plexus during a lying-down meditation. Allow it to bring suppressed feelings and past traumas up to be released, and show you what is stopping your spiritual growth. Then place it on the heart chakra to open you up to unconditional love. Add a gentler crystal to this process, such as rose quartz or rhodonite, as using malachite can mean intense mood swings and sudden change. If it causes heart palpitations, replace it with either of these stones to calm.

Because malachite absorbs so much, it needs to be cleansed regularly under running water. This gradually weakens the stone; when it eventually crumbles, bury it in soil, as its work is complete.

Moonstone

BEST FOR:
Boosting fertility of plants and women, easing menstrual or menopause symptoms, calming emotions.

LOOKS:
Translucent white, dusky pink, gray, yellow and sometimes blue, all displaying a pearly opalescence.

Looking like the moon shimmering in the night sky, this crystal carries the intuitive and feminine powers of our lunar guide and links us to nature's cycles. This boosts fertility and helps with menstruation and menopause issues, including easing PMS, fluid retention and hot flashes. For men, it helps them tune into their more feminine side, balancing aggressiveness.

Moonstone is said to lose its silvery sheen if the person using it holds too much anger inside them. It also changes color and should be used for different purposes according to the lunation. As the moon waxes to its fullest, moonstone will grow deeper in color, yet more translucent, and should be used for healing and manifestation. As the moon wanes, the gem will grow paler and emit more gentle energy conducive to rest and reflection on your inner world, calming emotions and soothing nerves.

Outside, use moonstone to help your garden grow well. Plant herbs or salad greens three days before the full moon—traditionally the peak growth time for plants—and bury a piece of moonstone with them to increase yield. Growing your garden according to biodynamic forces, using the lunar cycle, shows there is a right time to plant and the right time to harvest—in the garden and in life.

Moonstone has long been associated with love, especially in India, where it is given as a wedding gift to encourage harmony and fidelity between lovers. Made into jewelry in ancient Rome and Eastern European cultures, wearing moonstone is said to attract a new lover. Women meditating with it regularly will stimulate their kundalini energy and sex drive, and it's the biggest crystal booster of fertility.

Wearing a moonstone necklace when you make love at the time of the full moon should synchronize your body with the lunar cycle, helping you figure out your most fertile time to conceive. Or you could try making a fertility grid in the bedroom, with 12 moonstones in a circle around the bed and a 13th stone centrally positioned underneath. Moonstone in the bedroom generally encourages sleep and banishes anxiety and nightmares, especially for children.

For healing others, hold some moonstone close to your heart, filling it with loving energy, and then giving it to someone who is going through a tough time emotionally.

Orange Calcite

BEST FOR:
Boosting self-esteem and vitality, expressing sexuality and healing sexual wounds.

LOOKS:
Soft, warm light orange, waxy looking, sometimes banded.

Sunshine-colored orange calcite lifts the mood like no other crystal, dissolving problems, fears and depression. Legend says that orange calcite was thrown from the Baltic sun goddess Saule's chariot as she drove across the sky to begin the long journey to overcome the darkness at Winter Solstice on December 21st.

A balancing stone, it will increase confidence and self-esteem as well as motivate you to be more energetic in all areas of your life. Placed prominently in the home, orange calcite will clear it of negative or stagnant energy, and give everyone who lives there a boost of endorphins and positivity.

If your creativity or sexuality has felt blocked, orange calcite is the crystal to help heal this aspect of your life. Positioned on any of the lower three chakras when lying down in meditation, it will cleanse all three and energize your whole system, reigniting inspiration, enthusiasm and passion. Working with orange calcite is especially gentle but effective if there has been dysfunction, fear or trauma that has created psychological scars around your sexuality.

Meditate lying down with a piece of orange calcite above your groin area and visualize its vitality boosting your sexual energy and circulating around your whole body to radiate out into the world. It will help you and others embrace your sexuality, however it may present itself.

Women trying to conceive should carry orange calcite with them to balance their hormones and increase fertility. You may even want to create a fertility grid around your bed with a circle of orange calcite crystals surrounding it. This will also promote calm, restful sleep and turn stress into serenity, relaxing mind and body fully.

Placed on the abdomen, orange calcite can help heal the reproductive system and intestines, soothe kidneys and bladder issues, and alleviate symptoms of Irritable Bowel Syndrome. Make an elixir of calcite to drink to increase calcium absorption, boost the immune system, and stimulate healthy tissue growth. This can also be applied to the skin to treat warts, ulcers and wounds.

Recharge calcite as well as yourself by adding it to your bath and soaking by candlelight. When it crumbles, its work is done, so bury it in soil with gratitude for all of its healing help.

Rhodochrosite

BEST FOR:
Healing sexual abuse and emotional wounds, attracting new love or renewing passion, healing Mother Earth.

LOOKS:
Vivid raspberry pink, rose-red and orange, with swirls and circular patterned banding. Usually polished smooth.

Also known as "Rosa del Inca," rhodochrosite is only occasionally found in silver mines, where the Incan ruler Viracocha discovered it in the 12th or 13th century, in northern Argentina. According to the indigenous people of the Andes, the stunning pinkish-red stone was made from the blood of their royal ancestors, and was believed to be a stone of strength, stamina and powerful love.

Rhodochrosite's energy of love is more dynamic and intense than rose quartz. It encourages greater self-love and compassion, and will guide you toward happiness in love after pain or doubt. It is very effective at healing emotional wounds, post-traumatic stress and other issues after sexual abuse. Often known as the "inner child stone," it brings loving awareness to the truth of any childhood experiences. It helps you understand and forgive your parents or anyone else for mistakes, releasing the past so you can love confidently again.

When placed over the heart chakra in meditation, let rhodochrosite's peaceful energy fill your aura, heal your past and show you that you are deeply loved just as you are. By meditating often with this crystal, you will experience the blissful energy of universal love. This can also help with overcoming addictions that stem from having low self-esteem.

Use rhodochrosite to send loving, healing energy to mother earth. Tune in to the gem's power and ask: "How may I best serve the world?" Let your joyful ideas and inspired urges lead the way.

This healing stone contains manganese, which helps the body repair itself. Taken in an elixir, it can relieve ear or sinus infections, inflammations such as stomach ulcers, and other abdominal pain. If you suffer from migraines, try placing a piece of rhodochrosite at the base of the skull.

It is also soothing for skin disorders, including hives, rashes or shingles. Make a topical solution by placing a piece of rhodochrosite in distilled or spring water in sunlight for a few days to energize it. Heat the water gently and soak a cloth it in to dab on the affected area for a deep cleanse of the skin.

In a cave beneath the Andes, protected and revered by locals for centuries, there is a large, heart-shaped rhodochrosite boulder that legend says is the heart of Mother Earth, which beats once every 200 years.

The Best Crystals For Divination

Assess the present and read the future with a selection of carefully chosen crystals.

How to divine

Divination is the centuries-old practice of consulting the gods or goddesses—divus or diva—via tools such as runes or tarot cards to find out the best path to take, or what the outcome will be to a specific scenario. Using crystals for guidance goes back at least 5,500 years, according to the written history of early Mesopotamia—but even further back if ancient graves are anything to go by. Prehistoric people have been found buried with pouches of gems, crystal balls and polished crystal mirrors used for scrying. The ancient Greeks would use agate or jet to find out who was guilty of a crime, while Queen Elizabeth I sought the advice of her astrologer, Sir John Dee, who bought an obsidian crystal ball, with which he predicted the Spanish Armada invasion.

You can use crystal spheres, pendulums or a bag of smaller stones to help divine answers to pertinent questions.

✧ Cleanse your divination crystals before use.

✧ Whichever method you choose, first make sure to clear your mind of any worries or expectations. You need to be able to focus fully on what comes through in the present moment, and what your intuition is telling you. Tune in to your guides or a higher power for assistance if you wish.

✧ Take the time to carefully formulate the question you want to ask. Keep it as simple as possible and as close to the deeper core of what you want to know.

✧ Hold your crystals and connect with their energy. Allow them to harmonize with your energy so you can work together to get the best guidance. Ask them to show you the truth of the matter, clearly and with a timescale if necessary.

✧ Keep an open mind about the answer. Everything is possible. It might not be what it seems initially. Make a note of whatever comes to mind or is suggested by the crystal to look back at later and see if, on reflection, it makes more sense or is linked to what actually happened in some way. Take time to process your new realizations or answers, so you can make the right decision going forward.

Scrying with quartz and crystal balls

Crystal balls have long been seen as tools of personal wisdom, enabling sensitives to see into the future and make sense of the past. Scrying in crystal balls grew especially popular in 15th-century Europe, when people believed they could see angels or spirits within them to help divine the future. The most famous insight was that of Queen Elizabeth I's astrologer, Sir John Dee, who warned her of the Spanish Armada invasion after looking into an obsidian ball.

Whatever stone they are made from, all crystal spheres connect with the crown chakra and activate our psychic and clairvoyant powers, enabling us to access the Akashic records, where everything from all times—past, present and future—is recorded.

HOW TO READ A CRYSTAL SPHERE

1   First relax, ideally by candlelight, or use the light of the sun or moon to reflect into your crystal ball as you hold it.

2   Allow your energies to harmonize.

3   Ask the question you would like to have answered.

4   Sense any feelings, images or words that come to mind.

5   Place your ball down on a silk or velvet cloth.

6   Gently soften your gaze and look at your crystal sphere. It may appear to cloud over, but keep looking gently until any images appear inside the ball or in your mind. The different images may have significant meanings, or together they may make a story that serves as an answer.

7   When you've finished, disconnect from the ball and ground yourself in the present moment by taking a few deep breaths. Cover the sphere with a cloth when it's not in use.

8   Make a note of what you saw and anything you think it may represent, as well as what feelings or thoughts arose.

9   You can also do a similar reading with three smaller spheres for examining past, present and future.

10 For hidden insights into your past, or glimpses of former lives, look into an amethyst, rose quartz or calcite ball.

11 Then, to give guidance on the present connected to the past just seen, choose a sphere made of citrine or clear quartz.

12 Look into a beryl or smoky quartz crystal ball to see future opportunities or potential.

Ametrine

BEST FOR:
Concentration, connecting to
spirit and angelic realms,
uncovering and healing the
cause of disease.

LOOKS:
Sparkling transparent
stone with amethyst and
citrine combined, making it
shimmer shades of translucent purple and yellow.

Amethyst and citrine are naturally mixed together in this quartz crystal to make a unique combination that opens the third eye chakra, bringing deep concentration and spiritual insight for healing, meditation and divination.

In the 17th century, ametrine crystals were brought to Europe by conquistador don Felipe and given to the Queen of Spain as a thank you for letting him marry Bolivian princess Anahi of the Ayoreo tribe, whose father had given don Felipe the crystal mine as a wedding dowry. It later produced ametrine, and is still named after the princess. However, the gem didn't become popular until the 1970s and '80s.

Ametrine clears stress from the mind, so you can quickly and calmly focus during meditation. It brings higher consciousness into the physical realm, so it's good for insights and guidance that you can put into practice. It can also help lead you through astral travel, gaining wisdom while safely protected from psychic attack.

In healing and divination, ametrine gets to the bottom of things, including the root cause of diseases in the body and anxieties in the mind. Holding the stone will bring deeply hidden issues to the surface so they can be talked about and healed from. A great stone to help negotiations go smoothly and bring peace to warring sides, ametrine unifies the masculine and feminine energies within us all, and enables us to accept others more easily.

Place ametrine in your teenager's room to help them get out of bed in the morning and stay out of trouble.

Working with ametrine will enable you to contact spirit guides, angels and power animals, encouraging these higher beings to impart their wisdom and enrich our lives. Yet this stone also helps you take control of your own life with an optimistic and balanced outlook.

For a potent journey into the mind to uncover deeper truths, sit peacefully with a piece of ametrine in the light of a full moon. Imagine a door in your crystal that you can walk through into other dimensions. Visualize it in detail, seeing its shape, color and texture. Then go through that door into other realms such as the fairy forests or a portal to a past life, where you can see and bring back stories for contemplation later.

Emerald

BEST FOR:
Unconditional love, revealing the truth about relationships, stimulating clairvoyance and enhancing psychic powers.

LOOKS:
Bright green and sparkling transparent beryl.

According to legend, divine Egyptian magician Hermes engraved all the secrets of alchemy and magic on an emerald tablet. Consequently, it is believed to protect people from the illusion and enchantment of tricksters. In the Middle Ages, this much-prized gem was placed under the tongue to bring about prophetic visions of the future. Today, it is still thought to encourage clairvoyance and boost psychic skills, especially for older women.

Meditate with emerald to clear the mind and see a broader vision of life. Expect to sense a deep inner knowledge of the truth, have unconscious knowledge revealed to you, and receive the ability to discern what's right for you, along with the eloquence to express it. This calming crystal is also a useful tool for remembering past lives and the wisdom they hold for the present and future.

This green crystal of great beauty, connected to Venus, planet and goddess of love, symbolizes hope for the future, justice and security. Known as the stone of successful love, emerald promotes loyalty, unconditional love and long-lasting friendship. It is the traditional gift for anyone celebrating their 55th wedding anniversary. Wearing this gem, which activates the heart chakra, can heal relationship rifts, support mutual understanding and cooperation, and help reunite couples after a separation.

If you are counseling someone, or giving a psychic reading, use emerald to protect you from being overwhelmed with the weight of others' problems or issues. But pay attention if the emerald changes color in a reading, as this is believed to signify unfaithfulness in a relationship. Hopefully emerald's energy of renewal and harmony will encourage compassion and forgiveness, healing any heartache to appreciate what is.

Wearing an emerald will give you the strength to overcome any relationship difficulties or other trials in life, enabling you to love again with an open heart. But take it off at night, as wearing it constantly can make negative feelings rise to the surface. If this happens, however, emerald can also assist with positive reflection and renewed commitment to a higher purpose.

Iolite

BEST FOR:
Stimulating your psychic powers, creative inspiration and alternative views.

LOOKS:
Violet blue or indigo, and translucent, but becoming yellow or gray depending on the viewing angle.

A stone for enhanced vision, iolite was used by Viking explorers to help them find their way across the oceans. They used a thin piece of this color-changing crystal as the world's first polarizing lens to clear a hazy sky and enable them to see the position of the sun, even on a cloudy day, to help them accurately navigate on their travels.

Iolite stimulates the third eye, sparking clearer intuition, deep insight into your inner self and psychic awareness. It connects you to the higher realms for guidance and assists with past-life regressions. Lie down in a relaxed position holding a piece of cleansed iolite in your hand. Ask it to re-energize your aura and align your chakras. Then place iolite on your third eye to encourage a deep inner knowing and awakened consciousness. Let go of fear of the unknown and the need to control your inner experiences, and iolite will reveal the lost parts of your soul to help you move forward on your spiritual journey.

Alternatively, sit peacefully, gazing at a piece of iolite and letting its colors change as you move the stone gently in your palms. Breathe deeply and let it be your creative muse, allowing for unusual, otherworldly ideas and inspiration to come to you, and greater self-expression through the arts.

Known as the stone of witches, iolite is powerful in goddess rituals, to enhance creative spell work and increase your magical powers of manifestation. Often also used in shamanic ceremonies, the gem is good for going on an inner journey or vision quest to uncover the truth about your soul and your purpose here on earth. Pair iolite with onyx for spiritual protection and grounding, as working solely with iolite can make people feel out of their body afterwards.

Iolite helps you avoid distraction so you can focus on what is most important in work and life. In the workplace, it can encourage better brainstorming and different ways of doing things that everyone can agree on. If you are having difficulties connecting with people, it will help you see their hidden depths, or an alternative way of perceiving the problem.

Recharge iolite with natural light.

Lapis Lazuli

BEST FOR:
Prophetic dreams, increasing clairvoyance and inter-dimensional communication.

LOOKS:
Deep, royal blue flecked with gold iron pyrite pieces.

Twinkling like the night sky, lapis lazuli is made up of a mixture of stones including calcite, lazurite, sodalite and pyrite. Its celestial blue color was highly regarded by ancient civilizations, who believed it contained the power of the gods. It was used abundantly to make jewelry and as an ultramarine dye for the robes of priests and royalty. Many kings and queens of Egypt, including King Tutankhamen, had their tombs inlaid with lapis lazuli. They also wore it ground up as eyeshadow to improve their eyesight, as pictures in the Papyrus Ebers book suggest.

Lapis lazuli is a powerful stone for boosting your psychic powers. Place a piece on the third eye area in meditation and it will open up this chakra and enhance your clairvoyant and healing abilities. Meditate often with lapis and it will bring you inspired ideas in the form of visions, spiritual wisdom and intuitive guidance. Your dreams will also become rich with prophecy and meaning while working with lapis.

Lapis also balances the throat chakra, encouraging honesty and compassion in your communications, and releasing anger from past inability to speak your truth. Wearing lapis at the throat will help you face the truth of any matter with acceptance and grace, and enable you to share your opinion with others and encourage active listening, harmonizing conflict.

This stone is a strong protection talisman that stops and returns psychic attack to its sender and enlists spirit guardians to keep you safe, especially while undertaking any spiritual journeying in the mind. Meditating with it or wearing it anywhere on the body above the diaphragm will relieve stress and bring a deep sense of peace and serenity. It eases headaches, migraines and anxiety as well as calming the nervous system, and helps with any eye or ear problems. Simply hold a piece of lapis and send its healing blue light to the affected area, or place it directly on the painful spot and relax while it soothes.

If you are very attracted to lapis lazuli, you may have had a past life in any of the ancient cultures, including Atlantis or Sumeria. Use a piece of this crystal as a focus for traveling back in your mind to these past lives to see the galactic origins of humanity and communicate with beings from other dimensions.

Place lapis lazuli in your workplace to maintain integrity with your principles, inspire others' trust in you, and receive a promotion.

Onyx

BEST FOR:

Grounding, seeing the future, psychometric readings.

LOOKS:

Black with white banding or flecks like fingernails, most often polished.

Onyx is an ancient stone that was often set in the swords and armour of warriors to promote strength and vigor in battle. It was associated with wizards and magicians due to its use in scrying and spell-work, and is still used in rituals as a grounding stone. It activates the base chakra and creates a protective shield for anyone opening up their psychic side when giving tarot-card readings, providing mediumship or spiritual counseling, for example.

Using onyx to center your energy and align you to higher guidance at the start of meditation can leave your mind free to journey into the future to see what may happen. Onyx will enhance your intuition and instinct for what's right for you. Working with onyx encourages you to take full responsibility for your life, with confidence, stamina and strength to see you through even the toughest of times. Place a piece of onyx in your home to absorb any sadness, and stop nightmares and fear of the dark.

If someone wears onyx as jewelry, it can be used in a psychometric reading since it is believed to hold physical memories and will reveal the stories of its wearer to anyone sensitive to its energy. In healing, hold a piece of onyx, and it will guide you to a place on the body of a past-life injury. When positioned there, it will absorb the stored memory of that trauma and send universal healing energy to help.

Meditating regularly with onyx will encourage self-mastery, drive and wise decision-making. It will support you through any life changes by guiding you toward the best path for you right now. It can also help you concentrate better and keep a clear head, especially where there is conflict draining your energy.

Healing with onyx can bring you back to full health, especially if you've been working too hard or been through an illness, as it is believed to boost your immune system, cell regeneration and help your body absorb nutrients better.

Tune in to this crystal if you want to try channeling or automatic writing. As well as protecting you from unwanted energies, it will also bring you the clarity, drive and positive force needed for the highest messages to come through from spirits safely.

Recharge onyx in sunlight to boost its powers.

Red Jasper

BEST FOR:
Dowsing, nurturing ourselves and others, shamanic journeying, dream recall.

LOOKS:
Sometimes all one color from brownish, brick-red to a poppy-bright-red, or patterned with some brown or black inclusions.

Easy to carve, jasper was one of the most popular crystals to be made into seals and amulets. In Ancient Egypt, Mark Anthony had a red jasper seal ring with which he marked his letters to Cleopatra. To Native Americans, it was considered to be the sacred blood of the earth. These indigenous people found it especially helpful for tuning in to the earth to dowse for water, and many other cultures also revered jasper as a "rain bringer."

Known also as "the supreme nurturer," red jasper makes us feel whole again and want to help each other. Meditating with it feels like being wrapped in a comforting hug, perfect for grounding and relaxing you into a deep, meditative state. Hold red jasper during meditation or shamanic journeying to feel connected to and nurtured by Mother Earth. It will help you remember your dreams or imagery from any visioning, so that you can reflect on any information that may be relevant to your life at the time.

It aligns all the chakras and balances the masculine and feminine sides, bringing contentment and tranquility to all areas of your life. This alignment enhances astral travel, with each chakra's attribute playing a part in the astral journey. Place a piece of jasper on your solar plexus and heart chakra for protection before undertaking any out-of-body experience, to let it keep you safe.

Jasper brings determination and organization to projects, quick thinking and courage to tackle any problems, and honesty with yourself in all situations. In the home it will absorb negative energies including pollution and electromagnetic radiation.

Carry or wear jasper if you want to help others more, as it enables you to nurture yourself first and then share that love. This raises your awareness of your deeper needs and those of others, and the power you have to combat loneliness and isolation through reaching out. Use red jasper to increase passion in your love life, activate your imagination and help make your ideas a reality.

Jasper was used in the early history of the United States to divine the future; red jasper was used for visioning, and black jasper was thought to be good for scrying.

Ruby

BEST FOR:
Scrying, increased abundance, passion and energy.

LOOKS:
Various reds from transparent light red and raspberry to the most valuable, deep red with a blue tinge.

Shining bright red like the sun, rubies are full of our solar source's energy and vitality, which passes on to anyone wearing or working with them. Seen as more precious than even diamonds by the ancients, the Mongol Emperor Kublai Khan was said to have offered a whole city in return for a large ruby. They have always been associated with nobility and long-lasting love, representing the 40th wedding anniversary.

A powerful protector against negative energies, ruby encourages you to follow your bliss by opening the heart chakra and helping you enjoy the sensual pleasures of the physical realm. Ruby will bring passion and enthusiasm for life and love, attracting sexual partners to you by also activating the root chakra. It will increase your energy levels, motivate you to act on your goals, and fill you with a strong sense of leadership. With ruby, suppressed anger can be transmuted so you can move forward fearlessly. Thought to reflect the light of the soul, it also amplifies your innate talents and ability to succeed.

The ancients believed star ruby contains three angels or spirits to help you on your path. This variety of ruby has a six-pointed star naturally within it, on which you can focus your gaze to scry for wisdom about the past, present or future.

Sit in candlelight holding your star ruby. Look closely at the spot where the lines cross, and allow images to appear in your mind's eye or be formed on the crystal itself. These are symbols and messages from the Akashic records, where all wisdom and stories of all humanity are recorded. Sense intuitively what they mean to you. Or write them down and research their symbolism.

Many healers use star ruby, in particular, to integrate high vibrational energy into a patient's body, especially on a full moon when this gem's healing powers are even more potent. Ruby generally increases lucid dreaming, and helps you understand what you see in your dreams and decipher the meanings behind the imagery.

For an energizing meditation, lie down with ruby on your heart space. It will give your circulation, blood flow and lymphatic system a boost, increase your stamina, and fill you with dynamic life force.

Revitalize your ruby by wiping it gently with a soft cloth, then leaving it under starlight overnight.

Sapphire

BEST FOR:
Channeling wisdom and healing from higher beings, increasing psychic ability, manifestation.

LOOKS:
Sparkling, usually bright blue, but also yellow, green, violet and pink. Similar to star ruby, star sapphire has a star formation within it.

This powerful "stone of wisdom" has been the most prized of all crystals through the ages, for it brings spiritual insights, prophecy and good fortune. In ancient cultures, heavenly blue sapphire signified incredible celestial hope and faith. Buddhists believed it encouraged spiritual enlightenment, while Hindus would add sapphire to temple offerings to align astrological influences.

Initially used for spiritual healing, sapphire clears the mind and releases stress, aiding learning and understanding. It restores balance to the body and serenity to the spirit. With its ability to transform negativity of any kind, sapphire makes a powerful earth healer when used well, with enough focused intention and will during a healing session.

Sapphire can also be used to connect with the angels or source energy, possibly even extraterrestrial beings, and channel this higher consciousness for further healing of the body and mind. This power is even more amplified with healing chants, singing or music, adding gentle self-expression into the mix.

Star sapphire is believed to have the angels of faith, hope and destiny inside, known to share their knowledge with whoever gazes long enough at the intersection of lines in the pattern. Like star ruby, you can gain prophetic insight and increase your clairvoyance and clairaudience by scrying in this way with sapphire. It helps to focus your thoughts and sense the intentions of others, boosting your intuition and tuning into your own deep wisdom and truth. Working with star sapphire shows us that what we manifest is a reflection of our own essence, so keep it pure, kind and joyful.

The throat and third eye chakras are activated with blue sapphire, helping you stay self-disciplined on your spiritual path and to communicate your ideas, opinions, goals and desires clearly, and with focus, to fulfill them. Meditating regularly with this crystal assists in remembering past lives and knowing the lessons they've given you. It also assists with astral travel, so you can be transported to other places in your dream state, to bring back knowledge of all you've seen.

Sapphire releases any mental suffering or neuroses, including depression, bringing light back into your life. Its calm, balancing and healing energy encourages us into a happier life where all our dreams can come true.

Creating your own set of crystal oracle stones

Y ou can create your own set of divination crystals easily from a selection of different colored stones. Then you can choose a few at random whenever you have a question that needs to be answered.

Start with 11 at first, one each for the main colors of black, white, brown, gray, purple, pink, red, blue, orange, yellow and green. Pick smallish crystals of around the same size, all roughly the same oval shape and tumbled so they are all smooth. Keep them in a special drawstring bag so you can easily pick them out when conducting a reading.

Settle yourself somewhere comfortable and ask your particular question or state another's issue out loud. Put your power hand (the dominant one) in the bag and choose three crystals, one at a time—or ask whoever you're giving a reading for to do the choosing. Don't look in the bag, but choose according to which ones feel right or those to which you are physically drawn. Place the crystals you've picked in front of you to figure out their meanings.

As you add more crystals to your bag, whenever you find different hues of the same color, or the right size of stones, you can then choose up to six to give you an answer to your question.

FIGURING OUT WHAT EACH CRYSTAL MEANS

Hold each crystal you've chosen, in any order, in your cupped hands to tune in to their message intuitively. Close your eyes and let images or words come to you for each crystal. Start your reading with these impressions, and then see what each stone means according to common or ancient wisdom from the list below, including most of the crystals included in this book.

DAILY SELECTION

You can also choose a crystal each morning to give you a flavor of the day ahead or guidance on what will come. Carry it with you as a good-luck charm as you go about your business.

WHAT DOES EACH GEMSTONE MEAN?

AMBER

Your hard work may finally be recognized, and success is on the way. Take time to decide how you want to use it to your very best advantage.

AMETHYST

You're going through a big life change and have experienced stress recently. Be kind and gentle to yourself until you have more energy.

AMAZONITE

Be a leader and stand up for what feels right to you. You are in a powerful position to help combat injustice.

AMETRINE

Your intuition is strong, and you can sense that you need to step in to negotiate for others or stand up for yourself.

ANGELITE

Are friends or colleagues gossiping to get one over on the other? You may be called in to arbitrate and bring peace.

AQUAMARINE

Time to broaden your horizons with new friends and travel—either physically, or in the mind through expanding your spiritual consciousness.

ARAGONITE

If you've been waiting for more luck or freedom, be patient. Unexpected help is on the way.

AZURITE

Your psychic and healing powers are getting stronger, and you may soon be able to help others with them. Let your dreams and intuition lead the way forward.

BLACK TOURMALINE

Meditate on this confusing matter more, and you will get more insight and clarity about the best solution.

BLACK OBSIDIAN

You have a lot of power at your disposal as long as you don't mind making real change. Let past upsets go as happiness is on the horizon.

BLUE CALCITE

Stay calm and keep the peace right now, even with those who provoke and are hard to tolerate.

BLUE LACE AGATE

It's time to speak your truth on the matter and see what happens. The outcome is likely to be positive.

CARNELIAN

Believe in yourself and your
talents. Set your own goals and
work toward them, and you will
feel truly fulfilled and happy.

CELESTITE

Don't worry about what may or
may not happen. This stops you
from living in the present and
enjoying the now—that is where
the good will come.

CITRINE

Your creative talents may prove
prosperous, so communicate
your inspired ideas clearly. Now
is the time to try some new
activities that bring joy.

CLEAR QUARTZ

Time to be optimistic about
your health, wealth and
happiness. It's a great opportunity
for new beginnings.

EMERALD

You are successful and others
don't like it, but stay strong, as
their jealousy will pass.

FLUORITE

Clear: You will soon have more
clarity about who or what to
choose to make you happy.
Green: It's time to get in touch
with your spiritual self by
spending time around water.

GREEN AVENTURINE

Inspiration will strike you for a
new lucrative endeavor. Speak
up about what resources or
support you need to get your
idea off the ground.

HEMATITE

Make the most of the present
moment and new opportunities
will come your way. Don't fall
into old patterns of behavior
that block abundance.

IOLITE

There's more than meets the
eye about that new friend or
addition to the family. You can
afford to go deeper with them.

JADE

Compassion is needed for
anyone who is acting up. If they
are being difficult to deal with,
perhaps they feel inadequate,
unhappy or ashamed.

JET

You need to release pain and
anguish over the past, and
protect yourself from any more
negativity coming your way.
Take time alone to do this.

LABRADORITE

Use this time to travel on your
own to somewhere you've
always wanted to go. It's okay
to go it alone—this applies to
career matters too.

LAPIS LAZULI

Rise above pettiness by
sticking to your principles and
what you know to be true and
right for you.

MALACHITE

It could be a time for tough
love. You may be feeling under
pressure from others to act a
certain way. Follow your heart
to do what's right for you.

MOLDAVITE

If this situation makes you feel
disconnected from the material
world, fear not. You have a
unique path to follow and
special skills to share.

MOONSTONE

Are you deluding yourself about
something? Or are others being
deceptive? Pay attention to your
dreams and listen closely to
your intuition.

Index of crystals

Further reading

BOOKS

Cassandra Eason's Healing Crystals (Collins & Brown, 2003 & 2015)

The Crystal Bible by Judy Hall (Godsfield Press, 2003)

Crystal Healing Essentials by Cassandra Eason (Foulsham & Co Ltd, 2002)

Crystals, How to Use Crystal Energy to Enhance Your Life by Judy Hall (Hay House, 2015)

Crystal Prescriptions Volume 3 by Judy Hall (O Books, 2014)

The Complete Guide to Manifesting With Crystals by Marina Costello (Earthdancer, Findhorn Press, 2009)

ONLINE RESOURCES

www.crystalvaults.com

www.thecrystalcouncil.com

www.angelgrotto.com

www.kelseyaida.com

www.lonerwolf.com

www.fakeminerals.com

www.crystaltherapists.co.uk

www.thehealingchest.com

www.energymuse.com

www.healing-crystals-for-you.com

www.healingcrystals.com

www.crystalloverz.com

Tarot

Tarot

How to read the messages
of the cards

Alice Ekrek

SIRIUS

SIRIUS

This edition published in 2021 by Sirius Publishing, a division of
Arcturus Publishing Limited,
26/27 Bickels Yard, 151–153 Bermondsey Street,
London SE1 3HA

ISBN: 978-1-3988-1320-5
AD007324US

Printed in China

Contents

MAJOR ARCANA

MINOR ARCANA

Introduction

The tarot unlocks in the psyche messages from a vast, mysterious universe, one that may in fact be psychologically located in one's own subconscious. Modern tarot readers do not ask for their palms to be crossed with silver while they pronounce the swift arrival of a tall, handsome stranger. They are as likely to advise you on how to approach forthcoming challenges as they are to prophesize about what is due to happen to you.

The tarot's universal symbols speak of a journey; it is the one we all embark upon at birth, and it is our own personal heroic path through life. So, even if you are skeptical about the power of the tarot cards to predict the future, there is much to recommend them as a guide to discovering what concerns you have at the present time, lying just under the surface of your consciousness.

Some of the imagery of the deck can be worrying— the figure of Death cutting down souls or people falling headlong from a blazing tower—however, this should be considered in the manner of a dream after you awaken. You will not die (or at least not immediately after drawing a Death card), and you are unlikely to plummet from a high vantage point either. The Death in the card is one necessary for transformation and change to come about, and the people falling from the Tower are losing their

long-held, man-made beliefs—represented by the tower in the picture.

As you do a reading, remember that your fate is not predetermined and outcomes will change as you change your attitude, behavior and responses. A reading is a snapshot of what's coming in the next 6-12 months for you, and it is rare that a reader will be able to accurately draw cards for any longer period of time than that.

History of the Tarot

The origins of the tarot are not known, but evidence suggests that the cards, as we recognize them, have been in existence since the 15th century. The first set of tarot cards that we know of, the Visconti-Sforza pack, is Italian in origin; the second and more complete set is known as the Charles VI pack, named after the king of France at the time, although this deck may also have originated in Italy. The earliest evidence of playing cards in existence dates back to 9th-century China, so there are some who speculate that medieval tarot cards could have been based on these earlier playing cards.

Tarot cards are thought to have been used in card games known as *tarocchi*. The only firm evidence we have that they were used to divine the future dates from the 18th century, although there is fragmentary

evidence to show that they may have been used for this purpose much earlier.

The symbolic images on the tarot cards reflect the medieval and Renaissance European cultures from which they emerged. There were many multicultural influences in Renaissance Europe, including hermetic thought from Ancient Egypt and Greece, and other divination systems such as astrology and the Kabbalah – a school of thought in Jewish mysticism. All these belief systems would have had followers at the time, and the images on the tarot reflect this. However, although the cards are clearly rooted in the ancient past, there is a timeless quality to the symbolism that speaks to people across cultures today, and ensures their continued popularity.

How to use the cards

The choice of decks

Today there are hundreds of different tarot designs to choose from, many of which have a theme or specific purpose, such as answering questions about love and romantic relationships or catering to every interest, from pets to Arthurian legends. Given the wide range of choice, it can be difficult for the beginner to decide which type to select. Ideally we inherit our cards from a relative or friend, but many of us buy our own packs and let our instincts guide us.

The tarot we have used to illustrate this book is the Tarot of Marseilles, a deck from c.1650 France, created by Jean Noblet of Paris. However, interpretations often allude to the symbols found in one of the most popular sets of tarot cards – the Rider-Waite-Smith pack. Created in 1909, it was designed by artist Pamela Colman Smith (pictured below) according to the instructions of Arthur Edward Waite – an academic, freemason and prominent member of the Hermetic Order of the Golden Dawn (a group similar to a masonic order, but interested in magical and occult theory) – and produced by the Rider company. Originally called the Rider-Waite pack (but amended to include Smith's contribution), it is now the standard deck and has been

used as a template for numerous others. Each card has its own meaning, which is applied to the context of the question being asked as well as to the card's particular position in a spread.

When learning the tarot, it is advisable to understand the meaning of the cards and then develop your own personal interpretation as you become more proficient. This way, you develop your own intuitive system. You may also want to create your own deck of tarot cards and personalize them by using the images you associate with the meaning of the cards.

THE MINOR AND MAJOR ARCANA

The tarot deck comprises 78 cards, 56 of which are divided into four suits and known as the Minor Arcana. The remaining 22 are picture cards known as the Major Arcana. Arcana is a Latin word meaning "secret," "mystery," or "mysterious," and refers to the mysteries that the tarot helps us uncover.

The Minor Arcana cards correspond to the suits in ordinary playing cards and with the four elements of fire, earth, air and water as well as representing other esoteric qualities (see Table of Correspondence on page 14).

The Major Arcana cards are not thought to correspond to playing cards. They are often numbered from 0 to 21, although the order varies slightly depending on the deck. They're usually ordered from the Fool card at 0 to the World at 21.

TABLE OF CORRESPONDENCE OF THE MINOR ARCANA

Tarot suit	WANDS	CUPS
Playing card suit	Clubs	Hearts
Element	Fire	Water
Season	Spring	Summer
Timing	Days	Months
Qualities	action creativity energy enterprise intuition hope potential	love relationships happiness harmony sensitivity emotion fulfillment

THE SUITS

In a standard tarot deck, the Minor Arcana has four suits, each of which corresponds to a playing cards suit—the wands or batons (clubs), cups or chalices (hearts), swords (spades) and pentacles or coins (diamonds).

There are four sets of cards in each suit, and they are numbered 1 to 10, with the ace as the first card. There are also court cards in each suit, although the tarot has one extra court card: the tarot knight.

SWORDS	PENTACLE
Spades	Diamonds
Air	Earth
Autumn	Winter
Weeks	Years
ideas communication conflict struggle separation resolution change	money work talent reputation achievement stability material realm

THE COURT CARDS

There are sixteen court cards in the tarot pack; each of the four suits has a king, a queen, a knight and a page.

If a court card appears in a spread, it may represent an individual in your life who possesses the card's particular attributes. However, it can also represent qualities of the querent that need to find expression. The kings represent mature male authority figures who embody power,

paternalism, achievement and responsibility. Queens are mature, maternal females and, like the kings, are figures of authority. They embody wisdom, confidence, fertility and life-giving qualities. Knights are immature men and women who are rash in their actions and tend to pursue their own desires and interests at the expense of others. Knights indicate change and movement in a new direction. Pages refer to children or young teenagers of either gender and represent youthful potential, dreams and other characteristics that are hard to define. The qualities they embody are delicate and need to be nurtured if they are to develop. Pages are messengers, and indicate that news of some kind will be received.

ELEMENTS AND QUALITIES

The card suits also correspond to the four esoteric elements of earth, air, fire and water and their associated qualities (see Table of Correspondence on page 14).

TIMING WITH TAROT CARDS

If a particular suit is dominant in a spread it may indicate when an event is likely to happen. The wands correspond to springtime and action, so represent the fastest unit of time (days); the cups correspond to summer and represent weeks; the swords correspond to autumn and represent months; and the pentacles correspond to winter and represent a year.

CARE OF THE CARDS

Everyone handles their cards in their own way, but part of the ritual and etiquette of using a tarot deck is to treat it with care. Practitioners are advised to keep the cards clean and wrapped in a cloth or pouch, or in a box, and stored in a private place when not in use.

It is advisable to become familiar with your cards and handle them regularly to build up a connection with them. In general, only the owner of the cards should handle them. In this way, you develop a deeper connection, and when the time comes to consult the cards, it is like approaching a personal confidante for advice. If you give a reading to another person (known as the querent), you may ask him or her to shuffle or cut the deck, but the querent's contact with the cards should be kept to a minimum.

PREPARING THE CARDS FOR A READING

Before the cards are laid out, they must be shuffled. It is worth focusing your mind on the question asked by the querent while you shuffle the cards. Then cut the deck once or three times and lay it out according to one of the spreads. Alternatively, you can fan the deck out on a table and draw the number of cards required at random, placing each one in its position in the spread in the order you pick them. Some tarot readers leave the cards face down and turn each one over as they come to them during the reading.

Card readings can also be given using only the Major Arcana. The reader needs to separate these cards from the rest of the pack and shuffle them as normal.

GENERAL INDICATIONS

When many cards of the same suit turn up in a spread, it could show that a particular element or quality is influencing the matter. If Major Arcana cards predominate, it may suggest there are wider forces at work and that external factors will determine the matter. When mostly Minor Arcana cards appear, it may suggest that the matter is in the querent's hands.

Aces represent new beginnings and, depending on their position in a spread, may indicate that the answer to a question is "Yes." The court cards may represent people in our lives who have the qualities ascribed to the cards, or they may direct our attention to those qualities in ourselves.

TIPS WHEN READING THE CARDS

The tarot is a complex system of divination. As with other forms of divination, on a superficial level it is just another form of fortune-telling. However, the cards have a deeper significance than mere prediction because they offer insights into the forces that are work in your life and in your innermost self.

We should remember to approach the reading with humility, compassion and sensitive consideration for all involved—including ourselves, the querent and anyone else who crops up in the question or during the course of the reading.

The symbols should also be treated with care, and used to help both reader and querent gain insights that will be of benefit. Whatever the nature of the cards selected, the reading should never end on a negative note. If the outcome is undesirable, we need to take the advice of the cards and consider how we can work towards a better outcome. Sometimes the cards may indicate that our desire for certain things will not lead to the best outcome for ourselves. It may take repeated readings, with the same results, before we understand and accept this message.

Sometimes the tarot can play up and will appear to give readings that don't seem relevant to the question asked. In these cases, it is best to leave the cards for a while and start the reading afresh later on.

You have to work hard to get the most out of the tarot, but remember that words are no substitute for experience, and being guided by others is no substitute for using your own instincts. Surrender to them and you will be richly rewarded.

REVERSED CARDS

When cards are reversed in a spread, they can be interpreted as having the opposite meaning of the one they have when upright. However, some people only use the upright meanings of the cards. These are the meanings we will use here.

SELECTING A SIGNIFICATOR

A card can be selected to signify yourself, the querent and any other individual who may crop up in the reading. This card is called a significator, or signifier, and is usually the court card (page, knight, queen, king) that best describes the appearance and characteristics of the querent or person in question.

REYNE·DE·DENIERS

The querent's astrological Sun sign may be taken into consideration when selecting the significator. For example, if the querent is female and her Sun is in an earth sign (Taurus, Virgo or Capricorn), then the Queen of Pentacles may be chosen to represent her— particularly if she also possesses the characteristics of that card, such as generosity, practical talents and a strong connection with nature and the physical world. If not, then another card may suit her better, and this can be chosen as her significator instead.

The significator can be taken out of the deck and placed in the center of a spread, or next to the spread, to set the tone and provide a focus for the reading. Alternatively, the significator can be left in the deck; if the querent's significator then appears in the spread, it can be understood to represent him or her in the reading, or the qualities he or she embodies.

Tarot Spreads

Tarot spreads

A single card may be selected from the deck to answer a question, provide general guidance on present events, or serve as a focus for meditation. Alternatively, one of the spreads can be used to answer a question or give a general reading. There are many different ways to lay out the cards in preparation for a reading. Some of the more popular methods are listed here.

The three-card spread

1

The Lovers

2

The Sun

3

The Hierophant

One of the simplest layouts is the three-card spread. The first card is selected and placed face up—this represents the past. The second card is taken and placed on the right of the first card—this represents the present. The third card is placed to the right of the others—this represents the future.

SAMPLE READING USING THE THREE-CARD SPREAD

The querent is a young female in her early twenties. She has raised a question pertaining to a relationship that has failed. She is asking the cards to shed light on the situation, and bring guidance to help her move on from the heartbreak and give an idea of what the future might hold.

The querent has selected the following cards:

Card 1: the past

This is represented by the Lovers card, which describes the experience of a deep connection with another person in the past. One might surmise that this was an important relationship that has had a strong effect on both people's lives. They may have felt they had made the right match. It would not be surprising if such a connection was difficult and painful to lose. She is still pining for that lost relationship.

Card 2: the present

The Sun in this position suggests that the most important focus for the querent at present is herself and her own healing. Perhaps the relationship has awakened her self-confidence and creativity. She should concentrate on her creative potential right now and find joy and satisfaction through achieving her own goals and potential. This way, she will gradually heal from the wounds of heartbreak and regain a connection with the self that may have been lost or compromised in a relationship with another.

Card 3: the future

The Hierophant in this position indicates that the experience of the relationship has led to a growth in wisdom and maturity. A new perspective on the matter will be found. A lesson will be learned and will result in the development of a new personal philosophy and outlook on life. It may lead the querent to take a class or learn a new skill that will bring greater personal fulfillment.

Since all three cards are from the Major Arcana, we can surmise that greater forces are at work, and the matter is out of the querent's hands. Perhaps the failed relationship was inevitable in some way; the two individuals were destined to meet, but the results of meeting and being forced to separate will lead to necessary changes in the querent's life.

The Relationship spread

1 The Emperor
2 Queen of Swords
3 The Devil
4 The Star
5 The Empress
6 Ace of Cups
7 Two of Swords

This is a useful spread for interpreting your relationship to another person, be that your partner, your boss, a family member or friend. The cards are laid out as opposite. Since it is a spread for the relationship between two people, make sure you keep the person in mind as you are shuffling, and don't muddy the waters by thinking too much about the situation at hand. You may even find that what you thought was going on between you and the other person is the opposite, as in the case when someone is being aloof with you but secretly rather likes you.

1 What you think of the other person
2 What they think of you
3 The strengths in the relationship
4 The obstacles in the relationship
5 Where you are right now
6 What influences are likely to come into play
7 The final outcome

SAMPLE READING USING THE RELATIONSHIP SPREAD

A woman wishes to know where she stands with a longstanding on-off relationship with a man.

1. What you think of the other person

The Emperor here indicates that she feels he can be a bit domineering and arrogant, and attempts to railroad her into accepting elements of the relationship on his terms. This isn't to say that she doesn't think highly of him, as the Emperor is a born leader and can be charismatic and attractive.

2. What they think of you

Interestingly, the character of the Queen of Swords can be quite similar to that of the Emperor—she is analytical, strong and is brutally honest. This card in this position does show that he is attracted to her humor and her integrity, but the problems may lie in how similar the two are to one another.

3. The strengths in the relationship

The Devil in this position shows a degree of eroticism in the relationship that is healthy and strong. The two are clearly attracted to each other physically, and this aspect of the relationship is often what draws them back together.

4. The obstacles in the relationship

Alas, there are too many hopes and expectations placed on the relationship, whether by the querent or by the man she is asking about. This desire to have the relationship be what it isn't is blocking progress and frustrating each partner.

5. Where you are right now

The Empress card can often indicate a woman who is loved, and content in that love, which is odd as the querent is clearly not content or secure in her relationship with this man. It could be that this is another woman in the man's life. It is also a card of fertility, and may show an unexpected pregnancy about to be announced.

6. What influences are likely to come into play

An Ace of Cups here reinforces the news of a baby. It is good here to check cards in the position before and after to see if it is a baby between the two people in the query, or between one of the people and someone else. It seems likely here that the man has another relationship that will result in a child.

7. The final outcome

The Two of Swords is a card of self-defensiveness and of blindly fighting your corner. It seems as though this relationship is likely to hit some bumps—and one of those might be a pregnancy one!

The Horseshoe spread

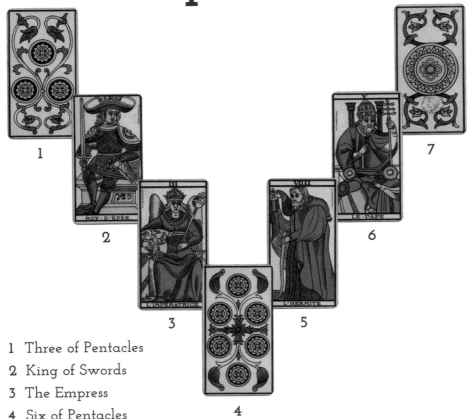

1 Three of Pentacles

2 King of Swords

3 The Empress

4 Six of Pentacles

5 The Hermit

6 The Hierophant

7 The Ace of Pentacles

For this spread, seven cards are laid out in a horseshoe shape (see opposite page). This spread is helpful if the querent has a particular question in mind; it can also be used to give a general reading of current circumstances.

The meanings of each card position are as follows:

1 The past
2 The present
3 Hidden influences
4 Obstacles that must be overcome
5 Others' perspectives
6 The best path to take
7 The final outcome

SAMPLE READING USING THE HORSESHOE SPREAD

A young man asked to have a general reading and selected the seven cards shown on the opposite page.

1. The past

The Three of Pentacles here indicates that the querent has been working hard and learning a trade of some kind. He has proven his skills and abilities to others and been recognized for his achievements in some way. Perhaps he is trying to figure out which direction to take with his career.

2. The present

The King of Swords in this position suggests that the querent is in a strong position of authority at this time. Perhaps his mental and analytical skills are being put to good use in his work as well as his private life. Or he may be in a particularly rational state of mind, able to think his options through and weigh them up to make the right decisions. He may be called upon to help others do the same. Being a court card, the King of Swords may also represent someone in the querent's life who displays these qualities and has an influence over the querent.

3. Hidden influences

The Empress in this position implies that a feminine figure has a hidden influence over the querent's life at the moment. Such a card may represent his mother or another female in his life. She is working for his benefit behind the scenes, trying to steer him in the right direction without his knowledge, and only wants the best for him.

4. Obstacles that must be overcome

The Six of Pentacles in this position may indicate that the querent's wish to share his wealth with others is holding him back in some way. Perhaps he needs to be careful with his resources and save for his future.

5. Others' perspectives

The Hermit in this position suggests that others may be thinking the querent is difficult to reach lately. He seems to have retreated from his normal activities and relationships to take time to think about his life and where he is going. He doesn't seem to have much time for his loved ones, and they are no doubt looking forward to hearing from him!

6. The best path to take

The Hierophant in this position suggests that the querent needs to figure out what is meaningful and important to him. Perhaps he will seek advice from a wise counselor who can help steer him on the right path. The querent has many questions about his meaning and purpose in life, and may need to take some time to get in touch with his thoughts.

7. The final outcome

The Ace of Pentacles signifies that the final outcome will be the start of new business projects and ventures. Perhaps the card points to the setting up of a new business, or to a job offer that's just what the querent was looking for. The purchase of a home, a sense of security and material comforts may also be indicated.

There are a number of pentacles in the spread, suggesting that career and financial matters are uppermost among the querent's concerns right now. Equally, the high number of Major Arcana cards suggests that there is a higher purpose at work; the querent can therefore trust that his path will unfold as it should.

The Celtic Cross spread

5

10

4

1

2

9

6

8

3

7

1   The Devil
2   Two of Wands
3   Seven of Pentacles
4   Ten of Pentacles
5   Page of Wands
6   Five of Cups
7   Six of Wands
8   The World
9   The King of Wands
10   Six of Pentacles

The Celtic cross is one of the most widely used tarot spreads today, covering general themes and providing a snapshot of a particular matter. In this spread, ten cards are laid out in the shape of a cross and a staff (see opposite page).

The meanings of each card position are:

1 The querent (a significator card can be selected for the querent and used in this position, or a card can be picked at random)
2 The obstacle or influences that have a bearing on the question
3 The question itself and the basis of the matter
4 The recent past—something that has just happened that has a direct influence on the question
5 The highest potential of the matter
6 The near future in relation to the question
7 Fears and concerns that the querent has about the matter
8 Other people's perspectives—how other people see the situation
9 The querent's hopes and wishes for the future outcome
10 The overall outcome of the matter

SAMPLE READING USING THE CELTIC CROSS SPREAD

The querent is a man in his mid-thirties. He has asked whether he should buy a property, but is unsure if he should take on the responsibility of a mortgage right now.

1. The querent

A card was picked at random from the pack to represent the querent in the first position. The card selected was the Devil. This does not suggest that the querent is evil! It means he has his own interests at heart, and will put his needs first in this matter. It may indicate that finding shelter is a matter of urgency, and the querent may find himself homeless unless the situation is resolved quickly.

2. The obstacle or influences that will have a bearing on the question

The Two of Wands in this position suggests that a lot of work and effort has gone into searching for the right home, and that the querent has now stopped to take stock. Perhaps he finds himself unable to move forward to make the decision and close the deal.

3. The question itself and the basis of the matter

The Seven of Pentacles in this position reinforces the suggestion that the querent is tired and weary after a period of hard work and research into buying a home. This may be deterring him from going ahead with buying a property. He is advised to stop for a rest and take stock of the matter before moving forward.

4. The recent past—an event that has a direct influence on the question

The Ten of Pentacles in this position suggests that material wealth and stability have been achieved. Perhaps the querent has saved enough money or received an inheritance that makes it possible to purchase a property. A wealth of personal resources is indicated by this card.

5. The highest potential of the matter

The Page of Wands in the position of the highest potential represents a creative spirit who calls for excitement and adventure. This card may represent the querent's own creative potential or it could be someone else who has influence in the matter. This card suggests that the querent's priority is not to get tied down in one place but to maintain a carefree lifestyle. For this reason, it does not look likely that the client will be purchasing the property at the moment.

6. The near future in relation to the question

The Five of Cups in this position suggests that the client's dreams and wishes may be dashed. Perhaps the opportunity to buy the property he has set his heart on will be lost and disappointment will follow. Or perhaps a relationship problem or breakup will affect his decision.

7. Fears and concerns the querent has about the matter

The Six of Wands in this position suggests that the querent is afraid of success! Everything he wants is within his reach, but this may be causing such anxiety that he is unable to move forward. The querent should consider why he fears the possibility of success. It may be that he is frightened of the responsibilities that come with it.

8. Other people's perspectives—how other people see the querent's situation

The World in this position suggests that other people think the world is the querent's oyster! They may believe he is in the enviable position of being able to do whatever he pleases and that limitless opportunities are open to him. Other people's opinions may be encouraging him to act cautiously to ensure he is not squandering the opportunities that are available to him.

9. The querent's hopes and wishes for the future outcome

The King of Wands in this position suggests that the querent has high aspirations. He dreams of traveling and seeing the world before settling down. The querent should follow his intuition and take the path that helps him realize his dreams and achieve his greatest potential.

10. The overall outcome of the matter

The Six of Pentacles in this position indicates that, after achieving his dreams, the client will be able to share his wealth and success with others. While his wealth may diminish slightly (it was the Ten of Pentacles in the past, now it has been reduced to the Six of Pentacles), he will find a way to use his resources for the benefit of all.

The majority of cards in this reading are wands, followed by pentacles, which means that freedom and discovery take priority over settling down into a stable routine. After the heartache that may be on its way in the near future (indicated by the 6th card placement), the querent will be free to pursue his dreams, and should follow his intuition in making decisions about the future.

The Astrological spread

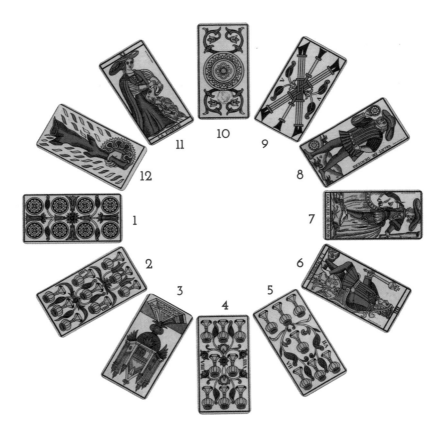

1 Eight of Pentacles   5 Seven of Cups   9 Five of Wands

2 Nine of Cups   6 The Emperor   10 Ace of Pentacles

3 Ace of Cups   7 Knight of Wands 11 Strength

4 Eight of Cups   8 Page of Pentacles 12 Ace of Wands

The astrological spread is based on the twelve houses of the Zodiac. It is laid out in the shape of a circular horoscope, with one card chosen to represent each of the twelve houses (see opposite page). If we compare the horoscope to a clock face, the first card is laid at nine o'clock, the second at eight o'clock and so on, in a counterclockwise direction, with the twelfth card at ten o'clock. This spread is often used to get a snapshot of the querent's current life, and can answer questions about various aspects, such as relationships and career.

The areas of life covered by each card position are as follows:

1 The querent's appearance and persona
2 Personal values and monetary matters
3 Communications and short journeys
4 Home and family
5 Romance, creativity and children
6 Work and health
7 Relationships and business partnerships
8 Shared resources, inheritance and secrets
9 Teaching, learning and long journeys
10 Vocation, career goals and aspirations
11 Friends, groups and community
12 Unconscious and hidden realm

SAMPLE READING USING THE ASTROLOGICAL SPREAD

The querent is a female in her early forties and would like a general reading about relationships and career matters. We can look to the 5th and 7th house positions in particular to describe relationships, and the 2nd, 6th and 10th houses for an indication of career prospects, although all the cards have a bearing on the chart. We should also look at each house position to get a general picture of a person's current experiences. The querent has selected the following cards:

1. The querent's appearance and persona

The Eight of Pentacles in this position suggests that the querent is working hard to achieve her goals and perhaps studying and learning new skills. To others, she might seem consumed by work and very serious about her career.

2. Personal values and monetary matters

The Nine of Cups in this position indicates that great wealth and emotional security are possible. Work is extremely satisfying and rewarding. If this does not describe the querent's current job, it should do so in the near future if the querent continues on her current path.

3. Communications and short journeys

The Ace of Cups in this position describes the ability to communicate with others from the heart. A new friendship or romance may begin as the result of a chance meeting while traveling. A love letter may arrive.

4. Home and family

The Eight of Cups in this position suggests that the querent needs some time away from her home and family to gain some perspective and learn to appreciate them again. It also indicates that it might be helpful for the querent to explore her family background and roots.

5. Romance, creativity and children

The Seven of Cups in this position points to the need to make a decision regarding a lover. If it is relevant, there may be a choice involving children. The querent may be feeling creative at this time and should listen to messages arising out of the imagination and dreams to help her come to a decision.

6. Work and health

The Emperor in this position suggests that a decision needs to be made about the querent's job. This could involve taking on increased responsibilities as well as the bigger decision about what job the querent really wants to be doing. The Emperor card recommends self-discipline and suggests that a father figure may have influence over the querent's decisions. The querent should make sure she fulfills her responsibilities at work and maintains a good healthcare regime.

7. Relationships and business partnerships

The Knight of Wands in this position represents a current partner or person about to enter the querent's life, who is fiery, courageous and brash. Perhaps the querent has had an argument with her partner that has resulted in angry scenes and caused her to question the relationship. The card might also signify that the querent's love life is about to take a new direction.

8. Shared resources, inheritance and secrets

The Page of Pentacles in this position indicates that the querent is being sensible with money and in matters that have been entrusted to her. She may be relied upon to keep a secret. In this placement, the card also suggests the querent has inherited a sense of responsibility and a strong work ethic from her parents.

9. Teaching, learning and long journeys

The Five of Wands in this position suggests a crisis in the querent's personal philosophies and beliefs. Perhaps the fiery arguments with her partner stem from this. The querent may need to visit a conflict zone or she may be met with hostility when traveling to a distant location. As indicated by the 1st card in the spread, she is currently working to develop a new skill, but may encounter obstacles that impact her learning. The problem needs to be addressed head on and a resolution found.

10. Vocation, career goals and aspirations

The Ace of Pentacles in this position represents great material rewards and achievements in the querent's career and chosen profession. Perhaps a new job opportunity or business venture is imminent. This placement indicates that the querent is on the right track to achieve her career goals and ambitions. Her hard work and diligence will pay off.

11. Friends, groups and community

The Strength card in this position shows that the querent is regarded highly by her friends and the wider community. While she encounters conflict in other parts of her life, the querent is in a strong position to work for the benefit of those around her, and may be asked to defend friends who are in need of assistance.

12. Unconscious and hidden realm

The Ace of Wands in this position is an interesting placement for such a lively and active card. It could suggest that the querent's intuition is particularly strong at this time, and she should use it to navigate the way ahead. She may also need to explore her anger, which may be rumbling beneath the surface and could be a reason for the conflicts encountered in her relationships.

Overall, there are mostly cups and pentacles in this reading, reflecting the focus of the question which was on relationships (cups) and career matters (pentacles). It looks as though important decisions need to be made in both areas, and that the querent has the diligence and commitment to succeed along whichever path she chooses.

The Major Arcana

The Fool's journey

The Fool

"I embark on my journey with trust and a light heart for the world opens up before me..."

KEYWORDS:

fresh start, beginning, freedom, courage, openness, trust, risk-taking

The Fool is shown standing on the edge of a precipice, bag and rose in hand, with a dog at his heels. He is stepping into the unknown, alone except for his trusty dog, full of expectation and potential and unfettered by the doubts and cynicism that come with experience. The card suggests a choice must be made and a journey started into unknown territory. Courage is required to take the first step. The Fool is unaware of, and unprepared for, what awaits him, but through new experiences he will discover his true potential.

The Magician

"*I am the master of my destiny and hold all the keys to success...*"

KEYWORDS:

skills, potential, mastery, resourcefulness, will, power, creativity, action

The Magician stands next to a table upon which lie all the implements of his trade. These represent the four tarot suits and the four elements. Wand in hand, the Magician is about use his powers to command his will. On his head, his hat is almost like the infinity symbol (explicitly shown in some decks), known as the cosmic lemniscate, which represents the eternal and immortal force of energy. At this first stage of his journey, the Fool realizes that he has all the resources he needs to gain mastery over the material world of opposites and duality. He has become the Magician, an authority figure who has the power to do good. Creativity and resourcefulness are needed to overcome obstacles.

The High Priestess

LA · PAPESSE

"*I am the seer who stands between worlds and makes manifest the unmanifest...*"

KEYWORDS:

wisdom, intuition, mystery, secrets, hidden knowledge, unseen influences at work

The High Priestess is also described as the veiled Isis. In the Rider-Waite-Smith deck, she is seated between two pillars, which represent the great universal principles and mark the entrance to the sacred temple. She holds a book containing esoteric knowledge on her lap. She stands for hidden knowledge, wisdom and intuition. When she appears in a spread, it could indicate that some hidden forces are at work in a situation, and that one must look inward for the answer. Trust in your own resources and ensure that your view aligns with what others suggest before you follow any external advice. The High Priestess represents the feminine principle incorporating the cycles of life and the creative force of the female.

The Empress

"*I am the loved and content woman, full in her power to give and receive love...*"

KEYWORDS:

abundance, pleasure, contentment, creativity, nature, nurture, balance, fullness, fertility, renewal

The Empress is Isis unveiled. Seated on her throne, she radiates the beauty that comes from harmony with nature. She is the great Earth Mother, in charge of the seasons, the fertility of the soil and production of the food that sustains us. At this stage of the journey, the Fool realizes that he needs to look after his health and physical needs.

The Empress indicates the possibility of marriage and motherhood as well as material gain. With careful attention and nurturing, a creative project will bear fruit. A situation is full of promise and has great potential to turn out as desired. It is usually a good omen to find her in a reading where the querent has a desire to manifest a good relationship.

The Emperor

"I am the responsible leader who always knows the right action to take..."

KEYWORDS:

judgment, decision, action, responsibility, challenge, effectiveness, satisfaction from achievement

The Emperor is the card of fathering, and indicates focus and the energy of accomplishment. The Emperor challenges the Fool to build something lasting to be proud of. The Fool is asked to make a decision about what he wants and what he values most in the world. He must then set out to achieve his goal. It will require hard work and unwavering determination and he will be judged on his abilities and the way in which he exercises responsibility. When this card is drawn, someone in a position of authority may offer advice that should be taken seriously and, more importantly, acted upon.

The Hierophant

"*I am wisdom in all its forms; heed me and prosper...*"

KEYWORDS:

law, tradition, religion, meaning, philosophy, teaching, learning, vision

Also called the High Priest or Pope, the Hierophant is a wise teacher, priest or counselor to whom we may turn in times of personal crisis. Like the High Priestess, the Hierophant is seated between two pillars at the entrance of the temple. However, unlike the High Priestess, the Hierophant represents the outer trappings and traditions of religious practice. At this stage in his journey, the Fool must find meaning and seek answers to questions about the purpose of his life. When this card appears in a spread, it indicates that we may be searching for meaning and need to approach a situation with a philosophical outlook.

The Lovers

"I will take you to the place of choice where decisions must be made for good or ill..."

KEYWORDS:

love, connection, sexual attraction, union of opposites, new possibilities, temptation, choice

In the card of the Lovers, we find a man and woman standing next to (and, in some versions, embracing) each other, with the man looking at the woman. The woman is looking up to the sky, where Cupid is watching, and, occasionally, such as in the Marseilles deck here, there is another standing next to them. The card alludes to love, relationships and the family, but the Lovers has also come to represent temptation and the need to make a choice. At this stage of his journey, the Fool finds his match, and decides to marry and unite the opposites within. The card suggests that a union is possible and that there is hope for a bright future ahead, if temptation can be avoided.

The Chariot

"I am the Charioteer who will guide you to your goal..."

KEYWORDS:

action, control, focus, strength, stability, willpower, conflict, struggle, change, triumph

The Chariot card represents gaining control over conflicting forces. The charioteer in the card is trying to control the two horses that are pulling the chariot. The horses—one red, one blue—represent principles pulling in opposite directions. The opposites that were united in the previous Lovers card must now be kept moving in the same direction. At this stage in his journey, the Fool must use all his strength to keep on the right track. By seeing what has to be done and taking control of the situation, obstacles will be overcome. If we manage to keep the opposite forces on the same path, we will go far. Events in the querent's life are moving quickly.

Strength

"I am the courage you didn't know you possessed..."

KEYWORDS:

strength, control, confidence, balance, integrity, courage, generosity, compassion

The card of Strength depicts a woman holding open (or forcing closed) the jaws of a lion, apparently without fear of danger. The lion represents our primal urges, the wild and ravenous beast within, yet the woman has succeeded in taming them. Like the Magician, she has an infinity symbol, or cosmic leminiscate, above her head in the shape of her headwear, indicating that she has achieved a new level of consciousness and understanding. The Fool is gaining mastery over the primal forces that have governed him, and his conscious ego is taking control. The card suggests that struggles may be ahead, but we have the courage and confidence to overcome any danger or challenge.

The Hermit

"*I walk the solitary path to find my way through to enlightenment...*"

KEYWORDS:

solitude, withdrawal, detachment, caution, patience, prudence, discretion, limitation

The Hermit stands alone on a mountaintop, holding up a lamp to light his way. He is wearing a cloak and carrying a staff to help him through the rough terrain. He has retreated from society to gain some perspective and look inward for answers. Through patient searching, he gains insight and connects with his intuitive knowledge. The Fool has reached maturity and questions his direction in life. When the Hermit appears in a spread, we may need to retreat from a situation so that we can recharge our batteries and have space to think. We are advised to retreat and figure out what is important to us before taking any further action in a matter.

Wheel of Fortune

"I am constantly turning so that which is low will rise again and that which is high will fall..."

KEYWORDS:

luck, chance, fortune, destiny, change, success, new direction

The Wheel of Fortune represents an unexpected element that will change the outcome of a matter. It may be good or bad, but generally indicates a turn of luck for the better and may herald opportunities and a new phase in life. Although we are responsible for shaping our own lives, this card suggests that luck and fortune may come along at any moment and change things for the better. When the Wheel of Fortune is drawn, an unexpected solution to a problem may present itself. Sometimes the card reminds us that "what goes around comes around," and that past actions will be rewarded.

Justice

"I am the balance that comes with fair reckoning..."

KEYWORDS:

fairness, impartiality, balance, reflection, decision, equality, truth, correct action

Like the High Priestess and Hierophant, justice is seated between two pillars, suggesting a religious connection. Justice is one of the universal principles upon which society is built. The figure in the card holds a sword and points it upwards, indicating that justice will be upheld. The sword of justice is famously double-edged, however, and a balance must be found between two opposing sides for there to be a fair outcome. This is represented by the scales held in her other hand. Following the Wheel of Fortune card, Justice reminds us that we are accountable for our actions, and urges us to be honest and fair. This card indicates that justice will eventually prevail.

The Hanged Man

"I am the sacrifice we must all make to arrive at the truth..."

KEYWORDS:

patience, waiting, surrender, sacrifice, wisdom, foresight, planning, strategy, eventual gain

The card of the Hanged Man depicts a man hanging upside down from a beam. His legs are crossed and he has reached an impasse. No further movement is possible for the time being. The card represents sacrifice and the willingness to face short-term losses to ensure long-term gains. The Fool must learn patience and how to act strategically to achieve the result he wants. He may also benefit from a different perspective on the problem at hand. An immediate advantage must be given up, but will eventually be replaced by a much better opportunity. All expectations should be surrendered for the time being.

Death

"I am the change that all must face in order to be born anew..."

KEYWORDS:

endings, loss, mourning, acceptance, adjustment, change, transition, rebirth, renewal

The card of Death depicts a skeleton with a scythe moving across a field of disembodied parts, most notably even the crowned head of a king. This suggests that the old order has ended and a new era is about to begin. At this stage in the journey, the Fool must accept approaching endings and uncertainty about the future. The endings may be difficult and painful, but we must learn to accept them. After a period of mourning and adjustment, we will be able to move on and embark on a new path. Change is inevitable. As we come to terms with this loss, we are transformed to enjoy a brighter future.

Temperance

"I am the key to keeping your head..."

KEYWORDS:

balanced temperament, harmony, moderation, cooperation, compromise, adaptability, relationship

The Temperance card shows the figure of an angel pouring liquid from one vessel into another. This indicates that feelings are able to flow freely. It may signify a guardian angel watching over us. The card represents balance, healing and harmony. The Fool has learned to master his thoughts and feelings and can now have harmonious relationships with others. We should act in moderation; compromise is the key to any problem. We have the ability to manage a situation and resolve problems. Events will run smoothly and success can be achieved. This card indicates that good relationships are possible.

The Devil

"I am the shadow you need to see the light..."

KEYWORDS:

lust, greed, rage, primal instincts, secrets, the shadow, success in career and personal interests

The Devil card may fill us with fear and dread because the Devil is a Christian symbol associated with evil. The card does not indicate evil, but asks us to confront the shadowy, instinctual part of ourselves. Following the perfect balance of the angel in the Temperance card, the Fool is reminded of those parts of himself that are self-serving and uncooperative, which he had tried to keep hidden—even from himself. When this card appears in a spread, things we don't like to admit about our own character and desires may be trying to break into our consciousness. We may encounter these unwelcome qualities in others or in our dreams. A neglected part of us needs to be heard. Personal gain and success in one's career is indicated by this card. We are advised to act in our own interests.

The Tower

"I am the crisis that is the making of you..."

KEYWORDS:

conflict, overthrow, disruption, disapproval, sudden and unexpected change

The Tower card shows a tall building that has been struck by lightning. It is in flames and about to topple over. The lightning signifies that the gods are angry or disapproving. The Fool encounters sudden and disruptive changes and crises that force him to question his journey. This card suggests that the times are volatile, things are not going according to plan and the old order is in danger of being overthrown. We should not try to hold on and save the toppling tower; it is better to stand back and wait for things to settle. We may face uncertainty for a while. This card asks us to re-evaluate our current path. A sudden, complete change may be the best way forward.

The Star

"I am hope, bright as Sirius in the night sky..."

KEYWORDS:

hope, faith, meaning, inspiration, promise, healing, protection, new horizons

The Star is a welcome symbol of hope, inspiration and rebirth to the Fool in the wake of the difficulties and uncertainties encountered in the Devil and Tower cards.

In this card, we see a star shining brightly in the sky above a beautiful woman who is emptying jugs of water into a stream. It represents feelings being returned to their source. Healing is possible and our sense of well-being is renewed. There is hope for the future and new possibilities are beginning to form. We are ready to give and receive love. The Star promises change for the better. This is a good time to meet new people, apply for jobs and aspire to what is really important to us.

The Moon

"*I am the fear that lurks at the bottom of the water...*"

KEYWORDS:

intuition, imagination, dreams, unconscious, fears, confusion, deception, disillusionment

The Moon is associated with night, the unconscious realm and the dream world, where our deepest fears and imaginations run wild. The Fool has encountered a period of confusion and disillusionment. Where is the promise of the previous card, and what does the journey hold next? Situations are vague and unclear; matters are not what they seem. We can act without being seen! We are advised to avoid deception and paranoia. At this time we can more easily tap into our unconscious and find creative solutions to problems. The way ahead is foggy, but we should allow our intuition to guide us.

The Sun

"*I am light and warmth and all good things to all people...*"

KEYWORDS:

joy, optimism, clarity, trust, courage, ambition, success, opportunity, health, vitality, happiness

The Sun, shown shining on twin boys, is symbolic of life in full bloom. The Fool has passed through his dark night, and the way ahead is clear again. He knows where he's going and what he wants to achieve, and he meets with success in all his endeavors. Indicating energy, joy, optimism and worldly success, this card suggests that it is the perfect moment to embrace opportunities and live life to the full. When this card appears in a spread, it promises good health, happiness and perhaps even the birth of a baby.

Judgment

"I am the one who judges the worth of those who come before me..."

KEYWORDS:

reward for past effort, re-evaluation, responsibility, outcome, resolution, acceptance

The Judgment card shows an angel, possibly Gabriel, sounding a trumpet above figures rising from their graves. It echoes the Day of Judgment referred to in the Bible, when Christ and his angels will return to Earth and even the dead will be judged on their deeds. This card can be understood to bring us the reward in life that we deserve. The Fool is forced to look at where he has come from, how he has behaved and the choices he has made. It marks a point at which we must re-evaluate our lives. We may need to learn hard lessons and be held responsible for past actions. We are advised to come to a resolution and move on with a clean slate. The card can also refer to judgments in law.

The World

"I complete the cycle that it may turn again and begin anew..."

KEYWORDS:
integration, fulfillment, achievement, completion, ending, final reward, success

The World, represented by a dancing woman, is the final card in one complete cycle. The creatures at each corner of this card signify the Christian tradition of the four missionaries—angel, eagle, lion and bull. These also represent the four elements and four suits of the tarot. The Fool has accomplished much and learned what he is capable of along the way. Challenges have been faced and battles fought and won.

He is now ready to resume his position at the start of a new cycle. New challenges beckon, and they can be approached with confidence.

All things will be possible for him in the fullness of time.

The Minor Arcana

Day-to-day life, people and experiences

"I am fire and speed."

Wands

Wands are associated with the element of fire, and represent sparks of energy and the life force. They are represented by branches that are sprouting leaves, suggesting creation, regeneration and potential for the future. There is a great deal of energetic activity in the wands, which translates into action—sometimes creative and sometimes defensive or aggressive. Many wands in a spread indicate that events are moving quickly. Wands are sometimes referred to by other names, including rods, staves, staffs and batons, depending on which deck of cards or book you use.

Ace of Wands

KEYWORDS:

beginning, change, opportunity, adventure, creativity, hope, action

The Ace of Wands signifies new beginnings and opportunities that can mark a change of direction in a person's life. There is the chance to embark on a journey or adventure, which may be sparked off by a new job opportunity, enterprise or relationship. The situation is full of hope and creative potential. It can also presage a birth in the family. Follow your intuition in taking up the right opportunities. Decide what you want to do, and act quickly or you may miss your chance.

Two of Wands

KEYWORDS:
rest after hard work, patience, trust, planning for the future

The Two of Wands indicates that a new goal or project is on the horizon. It has taken courage, care and determination to formulate your plan, so now you can stand back and allow it to unfold and grow. Leaving the matter alone to allow the magic to work can lead to a period of restlessness. Patience and trust in the future are required. At this time you should make plans for the next stage and figure out what to do once your creative endeavors have taken root and started to grow. Negotiations with others may be required. Travel may be indicated for you.

Three of Wands

KEYWORDS:

accomplishment, success, satisfaction, progression

The Three of Wands represents hopes and plans that have been realized in the world. Your ships are coming in and success is on the horizon. The first stage of a project has been completed and there is a feeling of great satisfaction and pride in your accomplishment. But remember, there is much work ahead, so you must not become complacent. Avoid arrogance and remember that you have not always been this fortunate and could lose your fortune again. The momentum of your success may propel you into the next stage of your project or creative endeavor.

Four of Wands

KEYWORDS:

reward, blessing, celebration, happiness, harmony, romance

The Four of Wands suggests that you can reap the rewards of your achievements. The card promises a time of peace and harmony. It is a temporary calm before the storm—more hard work and energy will be required again soon to resolve problems and conflicts that will arise. But for the time being, a great deal of satisfaction and celebration is in order.

Be charming and amiable, and enjoy sharing your success with others. Romance may be in the air.

Five of Wands

KEYWORDS:
fighting, conflict, obstacles, compromise

The fives of each suit mark the crunch points along the journey. The Five of Wands suggests conflict, as demonstrated by the fight scene depicted on some card decks. It can also indicate the possibility of lawsuits. In your effort to accomplish your goals, you have had to make difficult decisions and possibly cut corners, or stepped on other people's toes along the way. This may have been unavoidable, but now you must battle it out. Try not to compete, but find a way to resolve the matter; compromise, if necessary. You need to hammer out the problem and find a resolution. If you behave honorably, things could turn out to your advantage.

Six of Wands

KEYWORDS:

success, leadership, resolution, fortune, acclaim

In the Six of Wands, problems have been dealt with and a matter is on the point of being successfully resolved. You have the support of friends and colleagues in realizing your aims. Good news is on the way, so don't give up now. You should stay true to your original vision and goals. The card may indicate that you will receive public acclaim for your activities and efforts. Exams will have a positive outcome. Relationships are about to take a turn for the better.

Seven of Wands

KEYWORDS:

upper hand, position of advantage, challenge, force, reassessment

With the Seven of Wands you face another battle with others, but this time you have the upper hand. Remember to play fair, but maintain control over a situation and keep applying force. In the process you will learn to harness your competitive instincts to defend yourself and your creative endeavors. The challenges you face can also help you reassess your plans and goals, and modify your behavior as required. This will make you stronger and more successful in the long run.

Eight of Wands

KEYWORDS:

movement, progress, back on track, goals on their way to being achieved

The Eight of Wands represents a plan on its way to completion. You are back on track after a period of conflict and delay. Obstacles have been cleared and the way is free. You are focused on attaining your goals and forging ahead with your plans. Things are on the move. News may herald major changes in your life. Events are moving quickly and circumstances will soon change for the better. Things you hoped for will come to pass. Travel may be required to secure a matter in your favor.

Nine of Wands

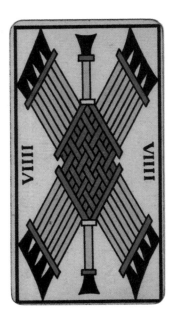

KEYWORDS:
final challenge, goal in sight,
perseverance, tenacity,
determination, courage to overcome

The Nine of Wands represents last-minute challenges on your way to attaining a goal. You have come a long way and are determined not to give up now. Although it may not seem like it right now, what you have been hoping for is within reach. With your goal in sight, you find the courage and tenacity to give one final push. If you persevere, no obstacle can stand in your way for long. From deep within, you must find the resources to keep going and remain hopeful. You have been given a final chance to prove you are worthy of success; it is up to you to rise to the challenge.

Ten of Wands

KEYWORDS:

achievement, attainment of goals, satisfaction, experience gained, rest and regeneration needed

In the Rider-Waite-Smith deck, the Ten of Wands shows an old man reaching his final destination. He is hunched over with the weight of his load. You have come a long way and are weighed down with the responsibility of turning your vision into reality. Your efforts are about to pay off, but at a cost, for you have been shaped by bitter experience and have lost the innocence and optimism of youth. As you reach the end of the cycle, you can find satisfaction in all your achievements so far. You will need to rest and recharge your batteries so that new ideas can form and you can start the process again.

Page of Wands

VALET·DE·BATON

KEYWORDS:
active, playful, imaginative, inspired, creative, youthful, folly

The Page of Wands is an active and boisterous youth with a fertile imagination. This card represents the urge to explore and play, to follow your dreams and look for new experiences and adventures. The Page seeks to avoid the responsibility that comes with maturity. When this card appears, it may represent a person, young or old, whose behavior is eternally youthful. It may also represent your own need to break from stifling habits and responsibilities, and develop these creative qualities within yourself.

Knight of Wands

CAVALIER·DE·BATON

KEYWORDS:
honorable, courageous, hasty, unreliable, aggressive, volatile, new direction

The Knight of Wands is a great warrior who loves to take risks and prove himself worthy. An honorable opponent, he defends the vulnerable and fights for their cause. He can be hot-headed and temperamental, and may rush to conclusions. The card may describe someone you know who fits these characteristics, or could indicate that you need to develop your warrior-like qualities to defend yourself or your loved ones. The Knight of Wands often signifies a move to a new home, or a new direction in life.

Queen of Wands

REYNE·DE·BATON

KEYWORDS:
strong, courageous, generous, vibrant, creative, wise, intuitive

The Queen of Wands is a wise woman, independent and authoritative, imaginative and intuitive, strong and courageous. She knows what she wants and how to get it. The Queen makes a warm, lively host who is generous with her gifts. The card may describe a woman you know who fits these characteristics, or may indicate that you need to develop these qualities yourself.

King of Wands

ROY·DE·BATON

KEYWORDS:

intuitive, decisive, active, inspirational, visionary

The King of Wands is a mature man of vision who inspires others. He has strong leadership qualities and uses his wisdom and powers of intuition to guide him in decision-making. Sprightly and full of energy, the King engages with life to the full. The card could describe a man you know who fits these characteristics or indicate that you need to develop these qualities of leadership, activity and inspiration in yourself.

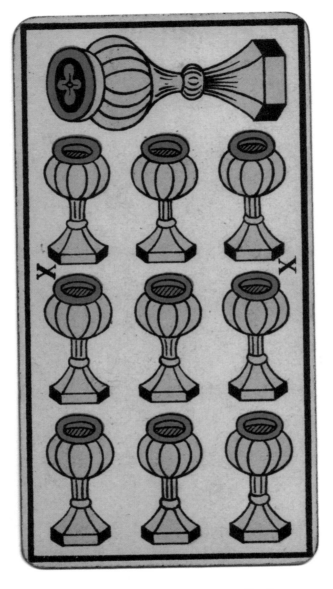

"I am water and love."

Cups

Cups are associated with the element of water and represent feelings, love, relationships and emotional fulfillment. They also signify the vast imaginative reserves within us and our unconscious realm. Water quenches our thirst and brings satisfaction and fulfillment.

The cups themselves are vessels for holding water, and they are often full (indicating fulfillment); however, sometimes the water has spilled (indicating crisis and sorrow) or is overflowing (suggesting abundance). Many cups in a spread signify that feelings and relationships are high-lighted. The cups are sometimes referred to by other names, including chalices, goblets and cauldrons, depending on which deck of cards or book you use.

Ace of Cups

KEYWORDS:

love, joy, happiness, abundance, relationship, emotional expression, fertility

The Ace of Cups, like the overflowing waters pictured on some card decks, indicates freely flowing emotions that need to find expression. There is potential for great emotional fulfillment. Deeply satisfying love and happiness are possible. The Ace of Cups represents the start of a new relationship, or it can indicate a marriage proposal. There is the chance of a fresh start and a new lease on life. There is great hope for the future—your emotions will sustain you and love will find a way!

Two of Cups

KEYWORDS:
new relationship, attraction, romance, harmony, satisfaction, conception, emotional fulfillment

The Two of Cups heralds the start of a new relationship, romantic attraction or connection with another person. You have the capacity for deep satisfaction and fulfillment. It feels as though you have met your match in another person. You see yourself reflected and mirrored back by your partner, and find out about new aspects of your character through his or her eyes. Existing relationships are strengthened. The card can indicate a marriage union or conception of a child, or perhaps another creative endeavor.

Three of Cups

KEYWORDS:

pleasure, joy, marriage, birth, feasting, merriment, celebration, abundance, fortune

The Three of Cups indicates that there will be a happy gathering of people. This card may herald a pregnancy or marriage proposal, or success in a creative endeavor close to your heart. You can be proud of your achievements. Joy and cause for celebration are indicated. This is a time to share your good fortune with others. You have renewed faith in the power of love.

Four of Cups

KEYWORDS:

dissatisfaction, boredom, discontent, depression, crisis, re-evaluation, self-questioning

For some reason you feel unhappy and discontented with your lot in life. You are in danger of developing a careless attitude toward life and becoming apathetic. You are entering a period of personal crisis and questioning, and have temporarily lost your connection with loved ones. You may feel that something is lost or missing from your life. The card indicates that you don't realize how fortunate you are. You need to take time to re-evaluate your life and decide what is really important to you.

Five of Cups

KEYWORDS:

loss, sorrow, regret, despair, betrayal, neglect, emotional breakdown, relationship breakup

The Five of Cups can presage a relationship or marriage breakup. The image on some decks shows a man in a black cloak turning his back and withdrawing from the world. Three cups have been spilled on the ground, indicating relationships that have been lost or thrown away. However, two full cups remain; this means you have a chance to hold on to whatever is left. You should think carefully before coming to a decision, for the effect could have consequences for yourself and your loved ones.

Six of Cups

KEYWORDS:

calm, serenity, acceptance, simple pleasures, nostalgia, old friends, new hope and opportunity

The Six of Cups is the calm after an emotional storm. Although things might not be perfect, you learn to accept your limits and find a new appreciation of those close to you and with whom you share your life. Your thoughts may be focused on the past, and you may start to idealize the "good times" as you remember them. An old friend may re-enter your life and help you come to terms with what you have become, bringing a fresh opportunity and a new lease on life. New friendships can also blossom. Hope in the future will be renewed.

Seven of Cups

KEYWORDS:

decision, choice, dream, vision, imagination, new path

The Seven of Cups suggests you are at a crossroads in life or in a particular matter. You have a very important decision to make, and there appears to be more than one option open to you. Each cup in this card is filled with a different option. You may rely on the imagination, a dream or a vision to choose the right path. But you are advised to remain grounded and realistic when working with the imaginary realm or your decisions will be short-lived and you won't be able to stick with them for too long. Think before you choose.

Eight of Cups

KEYWORDS:

retreat, escape, abandonment, loss, dissatisfaction, time out, perspective needed

The Eight of Cups indicates that you may need to go away for a while to figure out what is really important to you. You are unfulfilled and dissatisfied with your choices, and find it difficult to choose something and stick with it. Nothing seems to bring the satisfaction for which you are yearning. You must find a way to gain some perspective on your life before deciding what to do next. You may need to find a way to let something go and trust that things are on the right track. You may also need to lose something for a while before it comes back.

Nine of Cups

KEYWORDS:
wishes fulfilled, hopes realized, positive outcome, childbirth, joy, success, reward

The Nine of Cups is known as the "nine months card" and indicates the birth of a baby or another creative endeavor. Something you have tended and nurtured has come to fruition. You are brimming with joy, and the world is filled with hope again. Health and happiness are offered, and the problems of the past have evaporated. A wish will be fulfilled and things will work out unexpectedly well. You can enjoy your good fortune and find satisfaction in what you have achieved.

Ten of Cups

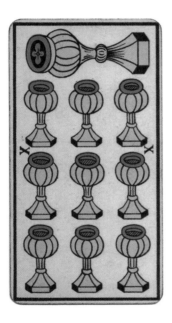

KEYWORDS:

lasting happiness, joy, fulfillment, emotional stability, fortunate outcome

The Ten of Cups is a card of emotional security and long-lasting fortune in matters of the heart. More happiness than you might have thought possible will be yours. The card indicates you have met, or will meet, the person with whom you want to spend the rest of your life. A situation has the best possible outcome. A stable, lasting relationship and family life are indicated. You can relax and enjoy the rewards of your efforts and good fortune.

Page of Cups

VALET·DE·COUPE

KEYWORDS:

sensitive, sympathetic, kind, imaginative, poetic, lazy, daydreamer

The Page of Cups is a sensitive youth—a kind, generous soul who is easily hurt, feels other people's pain and is sympathetic to their needs. The Page may be naturally lazy at times, and prone to daydreaming. He needs plenty of space to play and explore the imaginative realm. He or she may be oversensitive and may not take criticism well. News from a loved one could be indicated. This card may suggest a character who displays these qualities, or infer that these characteristics need to be developed within ourselves.

Knight of Cups

CAVALIER·DE·COUPE

KEYWORDS:

romantic, chivalrous, idealistic, questing, highly principled, on a mission

The Knight of Cups is the knight in shining armour of the pack, in all his romantic splendor. He rides around the kingdom searching for his love, ready to save her from any misfortune and ride off with her into the sunset. The Knight may also be on another quest—to seek the Holy Grail and restore the health of the King, bringing balance, peace and harmony to the kingdom. This card may describe a chivalrous young man or woman with a sense of mission and high ideals, or it may show these characteristics within ourselves.

Queen of Cups

KEYWORDS:

emotional, sensitive, caring, peace-loving, harmonious, imaginative, creative talents

The Queen of Cups is in touch with her feelings. Wise and peace-loving, she is in tune with others. She is sensitive, sympathetic and kind-hearted. A good listener, she can advise others on matters that are causing concern. The Queen is a highly imaginative woman with creative gifts and talents. This card can represent a mature woman in your life with these characteristics, or it can refer to these qualities in your own character.

King of Cups

ROY · DE · COUPE

KEYWORDS:
kind, honorable, responsible, respected, considerate, easily swayed

The King of Cups is a kind, honorable male who is trusted and respected by others. He is naturally caring and puts the needs of his subjects first.

A just and fair ruler, he has earned the respect of others. He can be easily swayed and manipulated, however, so may become distrustful of others' motives. This card can be chosen to represent an individual with these qualities, or it may highlight these tendencies within ourselves.

"I am air and ideas."

Swords

Swords are associated with the element of air and represent ideas, rational thought and communication. They concern the ideals of truth and justice. The swords are active principles, and the cards describe circumstances in which you are called to fight for what you believe in. Their blades are notoriously double-edged, indicating that every decision you make or ideal you support may have both beneficial and harmful consequences. Swords are made of cold, hard metal, suggesting a lack of feeling or emotion. A number of swords in a spread indicates a focus on thinking—you may be called to fight for, or be forced to reconsider, your beliefs and ideals. Swords are sometimes referred to by other names, including daggers, knives and blades, depending on which deck of cards or book you use.

Ace of Swords

KEYWORDS:

beginning, hope, ideals, principles, justice, conquest, new direction

The Ace of Swords stands for your principles and ideals. You have decided to embark on a new life or take a new direction, and you have high expectations of your future. Justice will be done. You do not wish to compromise your strongly held beliefs. The card may indicate the birth of a child, bringing great hope for the future. You are asked to have faith in yourself and your ability to overcome any challenges that lie ahead.

Two of Swords

KEYWORDS:

tension, balance, stalemate, difficult decision, action needed

The Two of Swords indicates that a matter is in the balance and a difficult decision must be made. You cannot decide between two options open to you. There is a suggestion that the way ahead is obscured. You must make a decision and stick by it. You should act now and not allow fears and doubts to hold you back. The sooner you make a decision, the sooner you can move on and find relief from a situation that is hanging over you.

Three of Swords

KEYWORDS:

conflict, struggle, heartache, disappointment, arguments, tears, separation

The Three of Swords suggests the experience of pain and disappointment in matters of the heart, perhaps because of a love triangle. Feelings may be sacrificed in the interest of rational thinking. Quarrels and squabbles with loved ones are indicated. A separation of some kind may result. In gaining some distance from the matter, you will find relief and realize that change was necessary in the long run.

Four of Swords

KEYWORDS:

rest, retreat, withdrawal, recuperation, relief from anxieties, rebuilding strength

The Four of Swords offers solace from a matter that has caused anguish. Something has been lost, and part of you feels as though it has died with it. You need time alone to contemplate what has happened and where things might have gone wrong. You must rebuild your strength and reorganize your thoughts before you are ready to face the world again.

Five of Swords

KEYWORDS:

unfair play, dishonor, belligerence, loss, facing consequences

The Five of Swords indicates unfair play and belligerent actions without consideration of their effects in the long run. You may have the upper hand in a matter, but your victory is double-edged and causes as much sorrow to you as it does to your adversaries. You have acted dishonorably and disobeyed authority to gain the upper hand. You must swallow your pride, approach a situation honestly, and be prepared to face the consequences of your actions.

Six of Swords

KEYWORDS:

solace, respite, retreat, healing, journey, insight, reputation restored

The Six of Swords may suggest that every ounce of strength has been sapped from you following a tough time, but the worst has now passed. The card indicates that a journey might be the best way to resolve a matter; this may be a journey in the literal sense or a journey of the mind. You are confronted with your subconscious thoughts and, as a result, insights may arise. You should allow things to sort themselves out without intervening. A matter that has been causing you great concern is on its way to being resolved.

Seven of Swords

KEYWORDS:

cunning, guile, deceit, tact, diplomacy, flexibility, compromise for the greater good

The Seven of Swords in some decks shows a figure stealing swords from a military camp. While such an act may be dishonorable, and your personal principles may be compromised, your actions may be necessary for the greater good. This card suggests that there are times when your beliefs and ideals must be flexible, and you should adapt them to the task at hand. Life throws many situations at us, and we can't afford to be too rigid in our thinking when we come to deal with them.

Eight of Swords

KEYWORDS:

restriction, mistrust, inability to act, indecision, imprisonment, isolation from others

The Eight of Swords represents restriction and mistrust. A situation seems hopeless, and you can't see a way out. You may feel trapped and hemmed in by your insistence on going it alone. You have run out of excuses, and of ways to avoid making a decision—there is no escape. You must learn to trust others, and should not be afraid to ask for help. You need to rebuild your connection with others and end your isolation before a decision is possible.

Nine of Swords

KEYWORDS:

fear, doubt, anxiety, nightmares, troubled conscience, suffering, despair

The Nine of Swords represents great anxiety and suffering. Your hopes have been dashed, you are filled with fear and doubt, and you struggle to come to terms with a matter. You blame yourself for an unfortunate outcome, but need to keep things in perspective. While it is necessary to face your part in a situation, you are only human and will make mistakes. You need to forgive and accept your limitations before you can lay the past to rest and move on.

Ten of Swords

KEYWORDS:

endings, misfortune, loss, defeat, new understanding, fresh perspective

The Ten of Swords represents defeat and marks the end of a difficult matter. At the end of a long struggle, something has been irrevocably lost. Ultimately, the outcome is not the one you wanted or welcomed. However, you must put the past behind you and move on to the next stage of the cycle. While you have been defeated on this occasion, lessons have been learned and you will move on with a new understanding of yourself, and a fresh perspective.

Page of Swords

VALET·D'ÉPÉE

KEYWORDS:

curiosity, intelligence, wit, honesty, independence, clash with authority

The Page of Swords is a clever, witty youth with a natural curiosity and inquisitive nature. He is in the process of developing his own ideas and beliefs, and may frequently clash with authority over differences of opinion. The youth's independent ideas and curious spirit should be encouraged and nurtured rather than quashed. This card may represent a boy or girl who displays these qualities, or may suggest that such gifts should be developed by the querent.

Knight of Swords

CAVALIER · D'EPEE

KEYWORDS:

fighter, warrior, reformer, prepared to make sacrifices for just causes

The Knight of Swords is a brave warrior who fights for the causes he believes in and is charged to protect. The Knight challenges injustice wherever he sees it, and shows courage against all odds. He is willing to make sacrifices to uphold his principles and fights for justice, fairness and reform. Change will be brought about. This card may represent a young man or woman who displays these qualities, or could suggest that the time is right for the querent to personally develop such characteristics.

Queen of Swords

KEYWORDS:
just, fair, intelligent, faithful, warrior, strong beliefs, idealistic, highly principled.

The Queen of Swords has a strong mind and keen intelligence. With a cool exterior, she may sometimes seem icy or aloof, but she is always kind and fair toward her subjects. The Queen will argue her opinions with a clear head and keen insight. She is not afraid to fight for her principles if her duties require it. When this card is selected, it may represent a female who displays these qualities, or may indicate that the time is right for these characteristics to be developed by the querent.

King of Swords

ROY · D'ÉPÉE

KEYWORDS:

intelligent, logical, fair, lawmaker, judge, counselor, warrior, strategist

The King of Swords is intelligent and known for his keen sense of logic and clear-headedness. He is an excellent judge and counselor to his people, and a capable warrior and military strategist. He has many innovative ideas, encourages reform and change, and runs an orderly, civilized society. When this card is selected, it may represent a man who displays these qualities, or could suggest that they should be developed by the querent.

"I am earth and abundance."

Pentacles

Pentacles are associated with the element of earth, and represent matter, the body and the physical world. Pentacles are concerned with material security and finances as well as personal values and the sense of security that comes from within. This suit also represents physical health and wellbeing, and the ability to draw comfort and satisfaction from personal possessions and the physical world. The pentacles themselves are in the shape of coins, suggesting money and earnings. Another word for money is talent; the pentacles represent talents and abilities that help us earn money and contribute to society in a useful way. Many pentacles in a spread suggest that material gain is highlighted in a matter, and practical action may be required. The pentacles are sometimes referred to by other names, including coins and discs, depending on which deck of cards or book you use.

Ace of Pentacles

KEYWORDS:

new venture, opportunity, promise of wealth, achievement

The Ace of Pentacles suggests a new opportunity or venture that will put our innate talents to good use. Like the other aces, this card represents high hopes for success and an opportunity to make something of our talents, provided we use them wisely. It also foretells the start of a prosperous time if it is drawn during a time of material lack and financial hardship.

Two of Pentacles

KEYWORDS:
balance, weighing up pros and cons, careful consideration, common sense, responsible decision-making

The Two of Pentacles is concerned with juggling two different duties, weighing up the pros and cons of a matter and making a carefully considered decision. In the image on the Rider-Waite-Smith deck, the figure balances two pentacles that are connected by the symbol of a cosmic lemiscate. This indicates that the figure must keep all his responsibilities in balance. You are challenged to make the most practical choice you can.

Three of Pentacles

KEYWORDS:
craftsperson, skilled artisan, recognition of abilities, achievement

The Three of Pentacles indicates that you will be recognized for your skills and achievements. Your handiwork is appreciated by others. You have worked hard and earned your success so far. While establishing a new venture, you have honed your skills and built a good reputation. Now you must reassess your goals and develop in a new direction. You can start another project from a position of strength. Financial affairs will blossom.

Four of Pentacles

KEYWORDS:

thrift, overprotectiveness, lack of generosity, mistrust, paranoia, isolation

The Four of Pentacles represents a withholding, ungenerous nature. You are afraid of losing what you have gained, so you hold on tightly to everything. You begin to become paranoid about other people's motives, and are so afraid of losing what you have that you lose touch with others and become unapproachable. This card can indicate a tendency toward obsessive compulsive behavior, hypochondria and a fear of taking risks. It warns that self-imposed isolation and the desire for total control mean you are in danger of pushing away those who love you.

Five of Pentacles

KEYWORDS:
financial worries, fear of loss,
destitution, failure, shame,
re-evaluation, starting again

The Five of Pentacles indicates financial worries and fear of loss or failure. It suggests both material and spiritual impoverishment. The card may presage the failure of a venture, loss of a job or redundancy. You feel you have not lived up to your high standards and expectations. Your fear of loss may have led to this situation. You must reassess your behavior and regain faith in your talents and abilities. You have the capacity to work hard, rebuild your reputation and achieve your ambitions.

Six of Pentacles

KEYWORDS:

success, sharing of wealth, charity, philanthropy, giving back to society

The Six of Pentacles signifies the sharing of good fortune with others. You have learned the lesson of the previous cards and now understand the consequence of holding on too tightly to material possessions. Plans are working out, you have succeeded in rebuilding your reputation in the world, and you can celebrate your success with others. Much satisfaction is gained from sharing time and money with worthy causes.

Seven of Pentacles

KEYWORDS:
rest after work, disappointing returns, re-evaluation of projects, redirecting efforts

The Seven of Pentacles indicates weariness after a period of hard work and suggests pausing to assess what you have achieved so far. It asks you to re-evaluate your plans and take stock of a situation. Are you on the best route to success? Perhaps you are overworked and disappointed with the rewards of your labors. A period of recuperation and regeneration may be necessary, and you might want to take a short break if you can afford it. You should not lose faith, but implement the improvements that are now needed.

Eight of Pentacles

KEYWORDS:

new skills, apprenticeship, confidence, job satisfaction, reward

The Eight of Pentacles represents acquiring a new skill. You may be learning a new trade fairly late in life. You are slowly but surely gaining mastery in your work and can reap the rewards of your efforts so far. Financial gain and job satisfaction are indicated. Faith in your skills and confidence that you will achieve your ambitions will help you stay on the right path.

Nine of Pentacles

KEYWORDS:

pleasure, self-esteem, humility, realistic evaluation, sense of achievement, satisfaction, windfall

The Nine of Pentacles indicates that you can take pleasure and satisfaction in your work and reap the rewards of your labors. You have worked hard to develop your talents and abilities, and have proved yourself a capable and worthy member of society. You are realistic about your limitations and recognize that you have had failures along the way. However, you can be proud of everything you have achieved so far and can draw great satisfaction from recognizing your journey to success. An unexpected windfall is also indicated.

Ten of Pentacles

KEYWORDS:

security, inheritance, lasting success, satisfaction, sharing, rewards, contentment

The Ten of Pentacles indicates that lasting success and material satisfaction have been achieved. You have earned the right to relax and enjoy what has been accumulated through your efforts. The card suggests that you have also gained an inner sense of security. In addition to your personal wealth, a family inheritance may ensure that you live in comfort for a long time. Enjoying the company of your family and loved ones, and sharing your material fortune with them, brings the greatest pleasure now. The card indicates a satisfying home life.

Page of Pentacles

KEYWORDS:

diligent, reliable, mature, loyal, steady, hardworking, responsible

The Page of Pentacles is mature beyond his years, and is the type of youth you can depend on: reliable and hardworking in his studies, and keen to start working from an early age. The Page of Pentacles makes a loyal, steady friend. A message about money may be received. The Page may represent a youthful person who displays these qualities, or may highlight the need to nurture these qualities in ourselves.

Knight of Pentacles

CAVALIER·DE·DENIERS

KEYWORDS:

sensible, considerate, stable, responsible, respectful, practical, nervous

The Knight of Pentacles is a practical, sensible, considerate character with a strong sense of duty and respect for others. Unlike the other knights, the Knight of Pentacles acts with caution, taking care not to rock the boat. Knights are normally very active principals who fight for change of some kind. This knight needs to find a way of balancing these two tendencies, or they will pull in different directions and lead to anxiety. This card may represent a young man or woman known for these qualities, or may indicate the need to develop them in our own characters.

Queen of Pentacles

KEYWORDS:

generous stable, sensible, down-to-earth, warm, comforting, healthy, contented

The Queen of Pentacles is practical, down-to-earth and generous with her gifts. She has an affinity with nature and animals, and radiates comfort and confidence in her body. She enjoys tending to her surroundings and taking care of others. She can be relied on to give fair, sensible advice and find practical solutions to problems. This card may represent a mature woman who displays these qualities, or can highlight the need to develop them in ourselves.

King of Pentacles

ROY · DE · DENIERS

KEYWORDS:

sensible, fair, honest, patient, generous, practical, traditional, stable, humble, self-reliant

The King of Pentacles is an honest, generous leader who has worked hard and achieved great success. He upholds his duties and traditions and respects his ancestral heritage. The King finds practical solutions to problems and dislikes experimenting with new methods and technologies, preferring the old way of doing things. The King is kind, but has high expectations of others and expects them to have the same self-discipline and work ethic that he has. He is humble and self-reliant. This card can represent a mature man who displays these qualities, or can indicate the need to recognize them in ourselves.

Index

Picture credits

All images Mary Evans Picture Library.